Carving Christmas Whistle Ornaments

Kelley Stadelman

Schiffer Publishing Ltd
77 Lower Valley Road, Atglen, PA 19310

Printed in Hong Kong

ISBN: 0-88740-973-3

Book Design by Michael William Potts.

Library of Congress Cataloging-in-Publication Data

Stadelman, Kelley
Carving Christmas whistle ornaments/Kelley Stadelman.
p. cm.
ISBN 0-88740-973-3 (pbk.)
1. Wood-carving. 2. Christmas decorations. 3. Whistles.
I. Title.
TT199.7.S7285 1996
736'.4--dc20 96-18196
CIP

Published by Schiffer Publishing, Ltd.
77 Lower Valley Road
Atglen, PA 19310
Phone: (610) 593-1777
Fax: (610) 593-2002

Please write for a free catalog.
This book may be purchased from the publisher.
Please include $2.95 for shipping.
Try your bookstore first.

We are interested in hearing from
authors with book ideas on related subjects.

CONTENTS

Introduction ... 3
Carving the Toy Soldier ... 4
Carving the Santa Ornament ... 23
Painting the Toy Soldier ... 37
Painting Santa ... 44
Gallery and Patterns ... 52

Introduction

As a child I can remember being mesmerized by the lights and ornaments on our Christmas tree. My imagination was uninhibited. I could picture the ornaments coming to life and hear the music that they danced to. I loved to play with them and put them into action. The ornaments in this book will allow children to interact with them in a new way.

They can take a variety of shapes and forms, as you can see in the gallery. In fact, the idea of making carved whistles is not limited to Christmas ornaments. A whole world of delightful carving may be in store for you.

The tone and pitch of the whistle is determined by the size of the hole. The deeper or wider the hole, the deeper the note. The shorter the hole the higher the note. Because of this different sizes of the ornaments and the way they are made into whistles can create a wide range of tones or, as in the case of the soldier carved here, even dual tones.

It is a simple task to make a whistle, and the steps are clearly demonstrated in this book. It may, however, be difficult to get the whistle part to work, and may take a little practice to get right. If you are concerned about ruining your carving practice the technique on pieces of scrap before working on the ornament.

I hope you have as much fun creating these Christmas charmers as I have. Feel free to inquire about paint color, pre-cut sugar pine blanks or any other concerns by writing or calling:

Kelley S. Stadelman
P.O. Box 191
North Plains, Oregon 97133
(503)647-0892

Carving Tools and Terms

Chisel: A tool with a flat cutting edge. It may have a single or double bevel.

Skew Chisel: This chisel has a double bevel and is slanted obliquely along the chisel edge.

Gouge: A tool with a single bevel and a cutting edge that is curved or shaped in a compound configuration.

Bench Knife: A carving tool with the cutting edge parallel to the handle.

Disposable blades: These blades fit into a special handle. They are made of thin metal and are extremely sharp. Generally they are not resharpened.

Care of Tools

After investing in quality tools, care should be taken to maintain their sharpness. Contact between your tools and surfaces other than wood may chip and dull them. Most towns have fine cutlery stores which provide sharpening services. However, I am of the opinion that the art of sharpening should be learned by every carver. There are several books that will give you instructions in the techniques of sharpening.

Carving Safety

Remember, you are using a sharp tool. You may become comfortable with carving tools in your hand, but they are obviously more dangerous than a pen or a paint brush. I have held a paint brush in my mouth, scratched my head with one, and even used on as a pointer. Doing these common gestures with a carving tool could cause harm to you or someone else. Protect yourself and your carving companions. Avoid pointing or talking with your hands with a carving tool in hand. Avoid placing tools on the table top so that they might roll off the table and onto (or into) someone's foot.

Whenever possible carve on the table top, not in your lap. Build up your chair with a pillow or two so you are well above your carving. Place your wood in a clamp or on some type of device to hold it in place. I like to use the non-skid grid that is used under throw rugs.

I have cut myself. I do not cut myself often anymore. I have a good sense for what my tools and wood will do. Carving when you are tired or tense will increase the chance of being cut. Take many little breaks. Know your limits. Be careful and have a good time!

Carving the Toy Soldier

Cut the pattern from stock that is 1-1/2" thick.

This ornament will have two whistles. We need to decide where the holes will be drilled to incorporate them into the design. Looking at the side I know the boots will be shaped something like this.

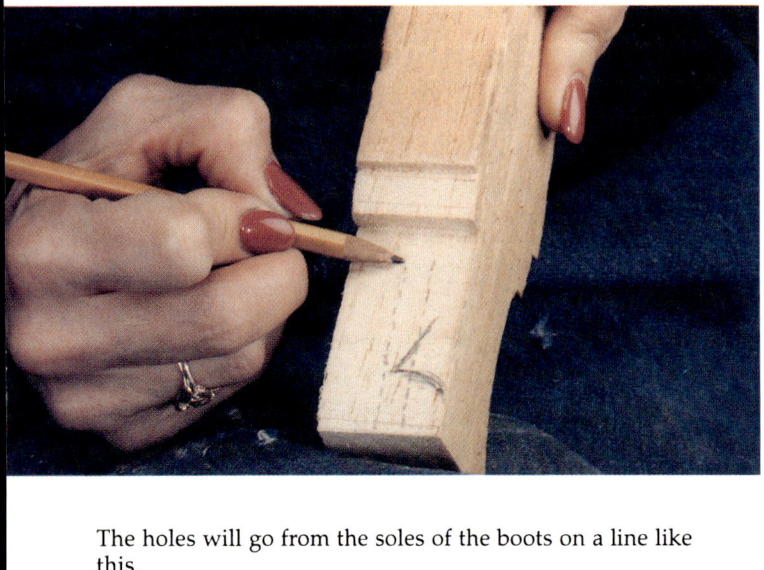

The holes will go from the soles of the boots on a line like this.

Where they cross the open area is where the reed of the whistle will go.

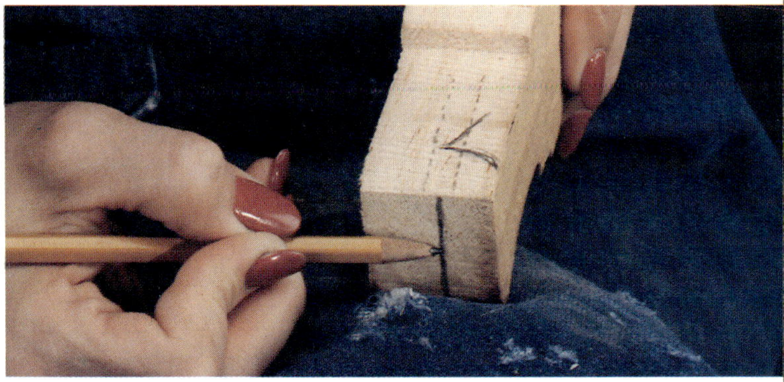

From the center of the hole line, carry a line across the bottom. The centers of the holes will be on this line.

Draw a midline across the bottom to intersect the first line, then center the drill entry points in each half of the base.

Use a drill press to make 1/4" holes as deep as the bit will go. In this case I have two holes for two tones, and to make them different sounding I leave one hole a little shallower than the other. The shorter the hole, the higher the tone.

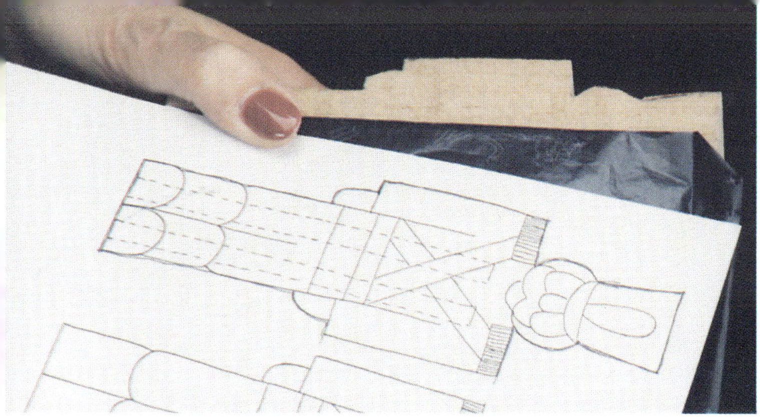

Transfer the patterns to the front and back of the blank, using carbon paper.

Knock off the corners, front…

and back.

Before carving the whole figure I need to get the whistle working. It is important to establish that before I go ahead and carve every thing else. Start by carving the reed. Draw the line between the leg and at the top of the shoe.

Score across the top of the shoe.

Cut back to the top of the shoe from the front of the legs.

Repeat as necessary.

The top of the shoe should be straight up and down.

I angle the reed back toward this at about a 30 degree angle, which I then adjust for the best whistle sound. Sometimes it ends up being as much as 45 degrees.

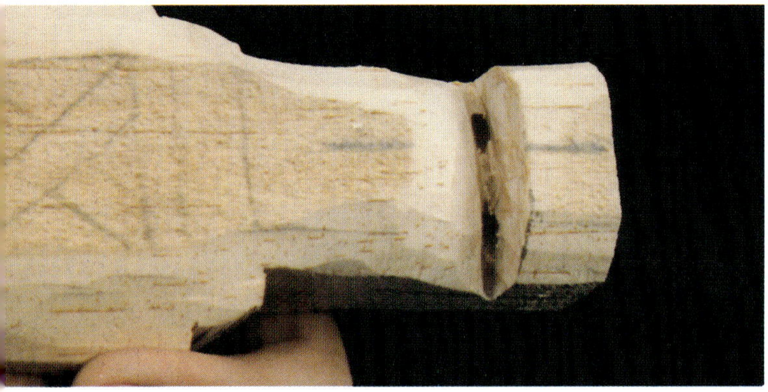

The wedge needs to go deep enough to expose about half of the holes.

Cut a length of 1/4" dowel long enough to go from the bottom of the feet to just past the wedge.

At the end, mark the top 1/3" of the dowel...

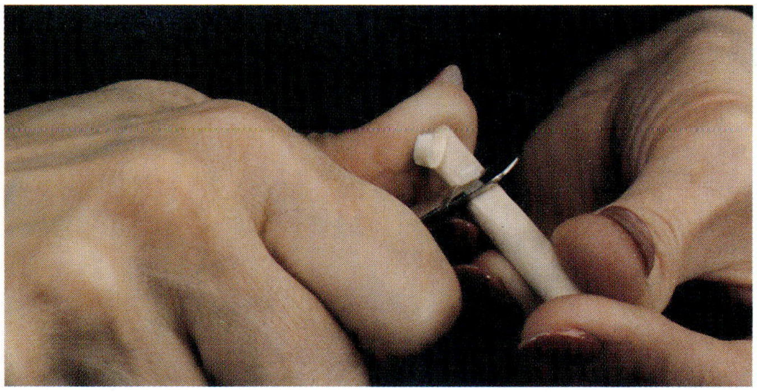

and trim the top surface of the dowel until it is flat.

Insert the dowels, flat side up, so that the ends are just flush with the straight cut at the top of the feet.

Test the whistle by blowing.

If it doesn't whistle push the dowel in a little further. Test it again and adjust.

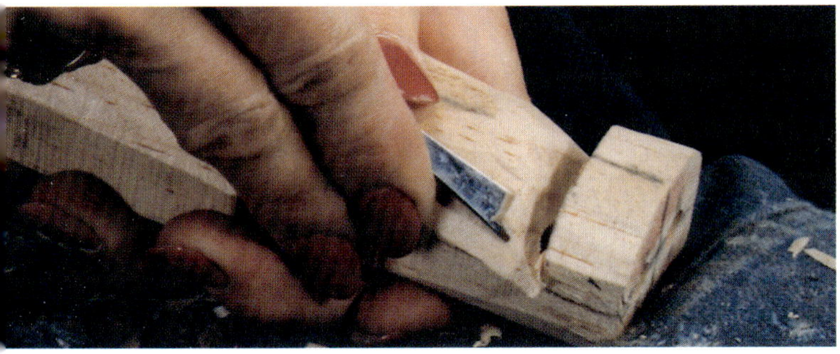

If it doesn't work this time you need to adjust the angle. Do this in small steps, taking off only a little between tests.

Test it again.

When the whistle works, reestablish the lines

Separate the legs with a v-tool. After all the work to make it whistle, you need to be careful not to carve the lower leg too much, especially in the area of the reed.

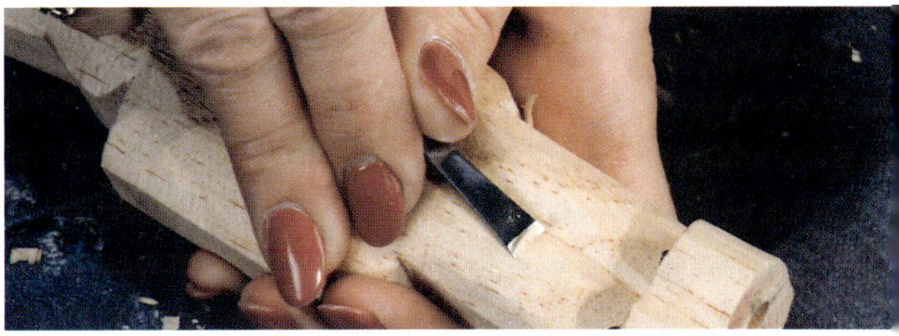

Work out from the vee channel to shape the legs.

Shape the top of the shoe.

Shape the backs of the legs in the same way. First separate them with a v-tool.

Then round them.

Establish the separation of the arm from the body with a v-tool. I always start in the arm pit and go down the arm. If you go in the other direction it is easy to end up with the armpit at the shoulder.

When the v-groove is set, I put one corner of a straight chisel in the bottom of the groove and start working the arm back.

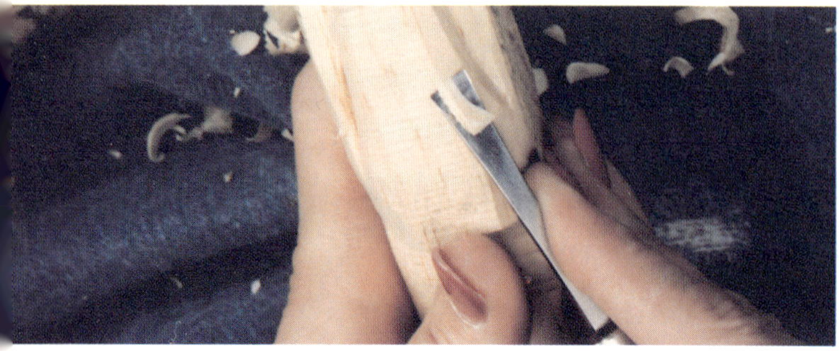

Check the width from the side, and start shaping the arm.

Under cut the inside edge of the arm a little bit to separate it from the body.

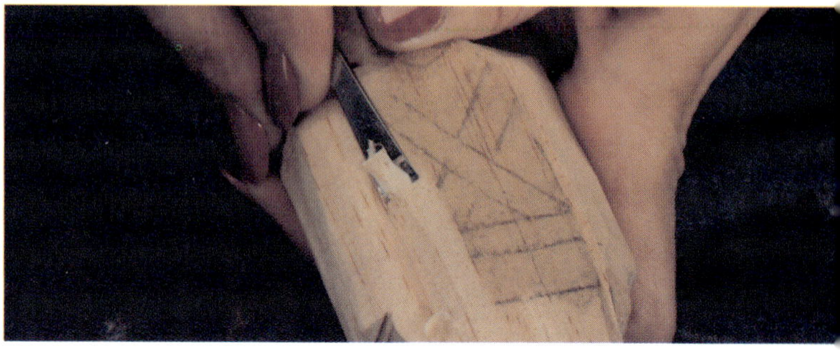

Shape the body a little.

Draw in the edges of the hands.

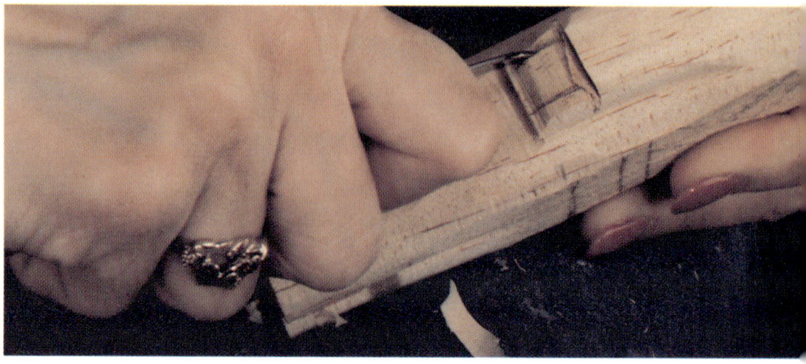

Score down the edges of the hand...

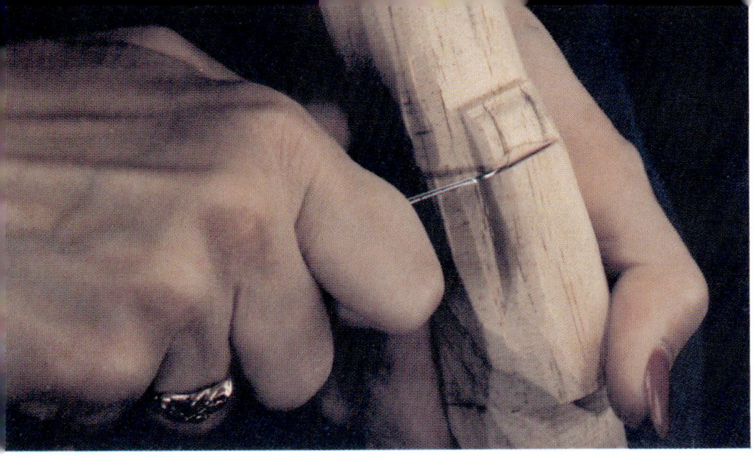

and at the cuff.

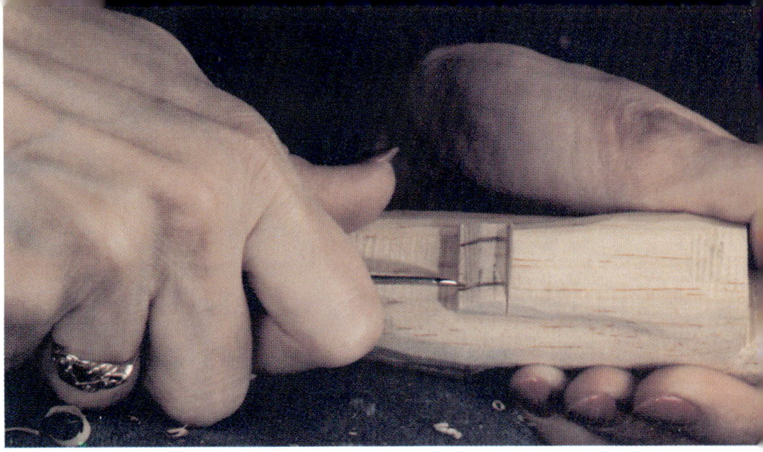

Do the other hand in the same way.

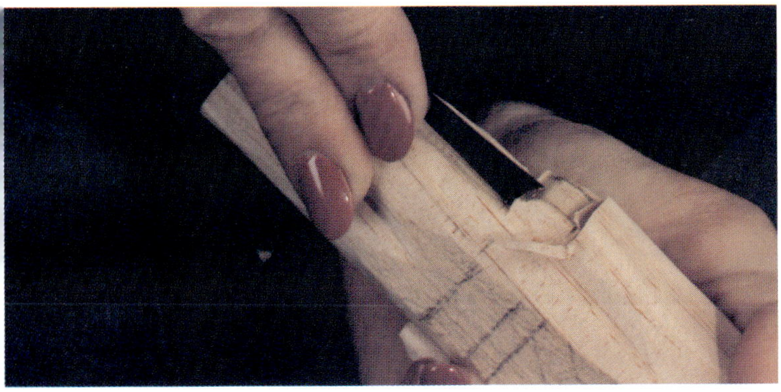

Remove the excess.

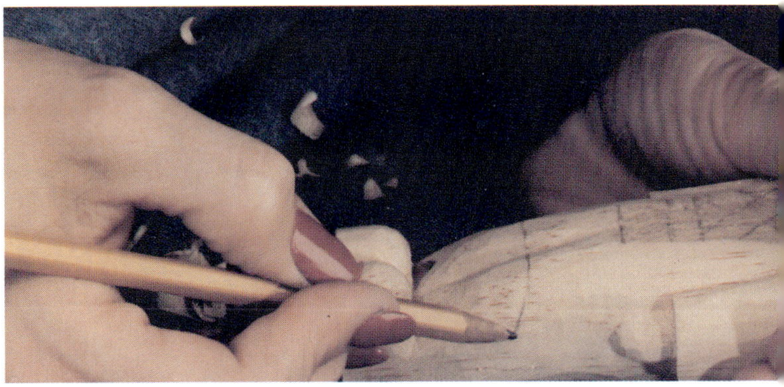

Draw in the line of the boots.

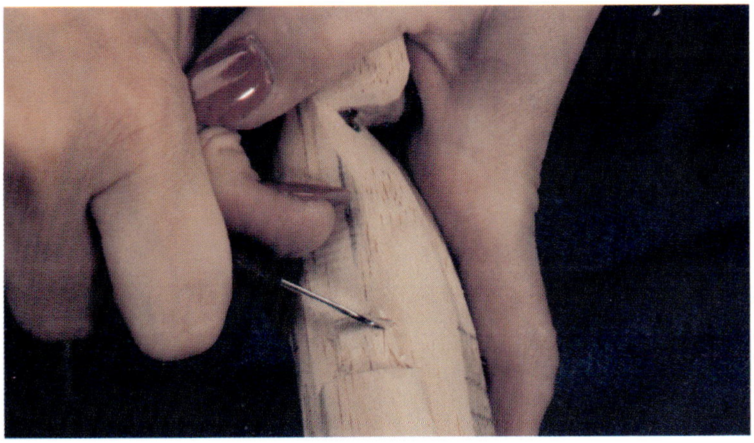

Shape the hand.

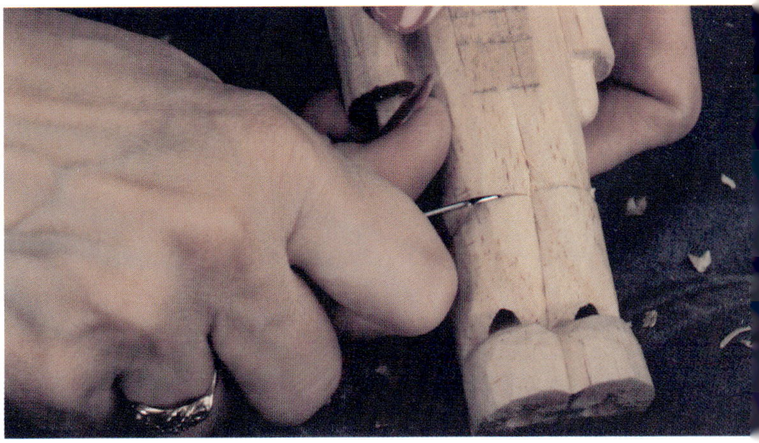

Score the top of the boot.

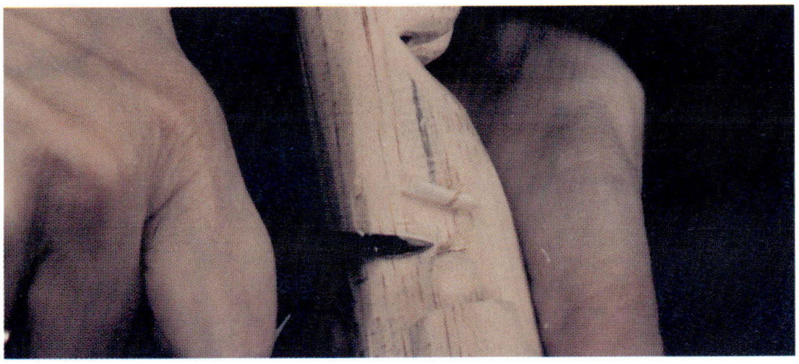

Clean up any rough areas of the leg and surrounding areas.

Trim the leg back to the boot.

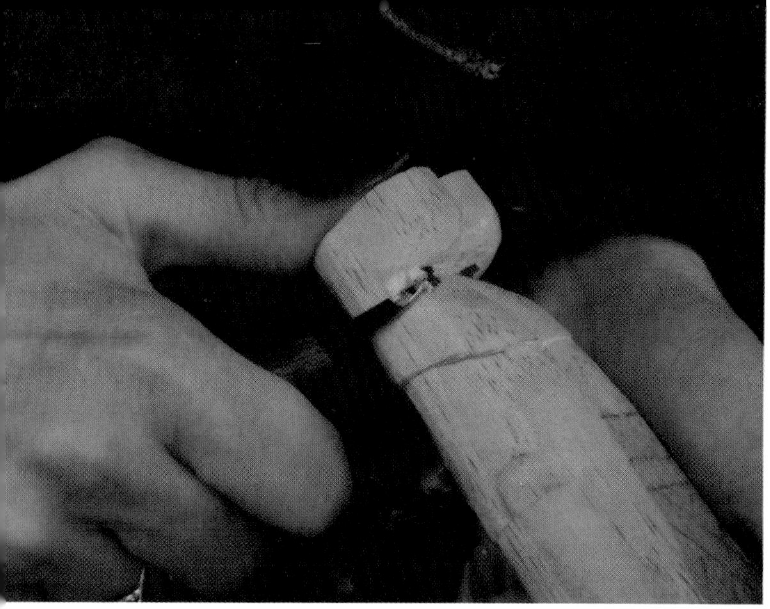

Refine the boots as you go.

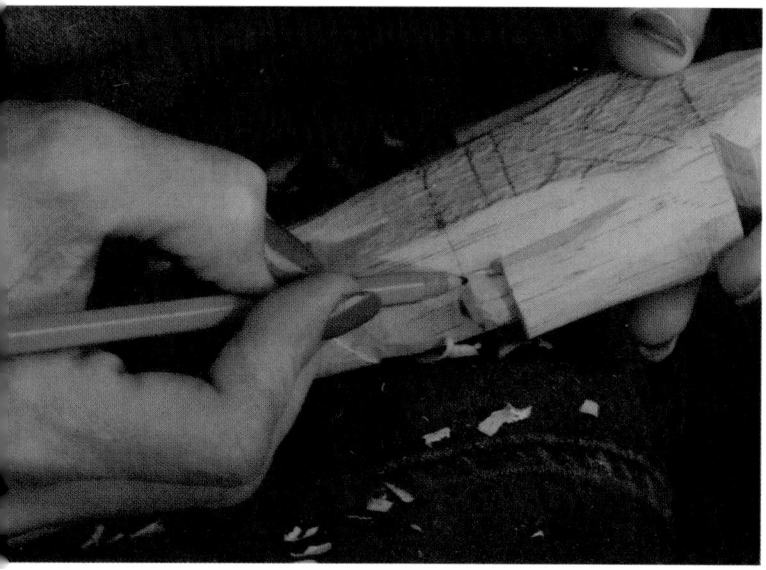

Reestablish the line of the bottom of the jacket.

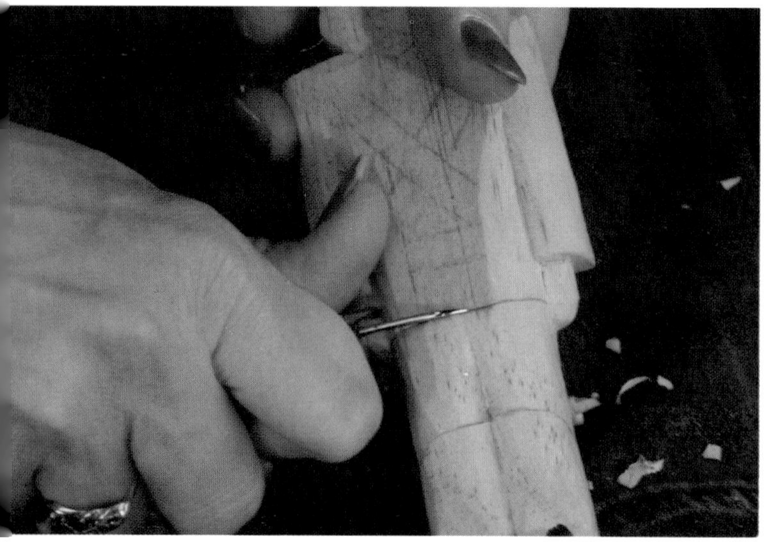

Score the line...

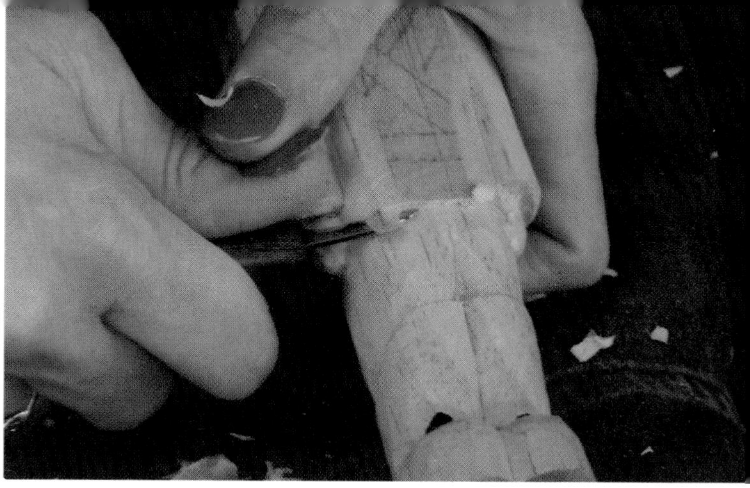

and trim the pants back to it.

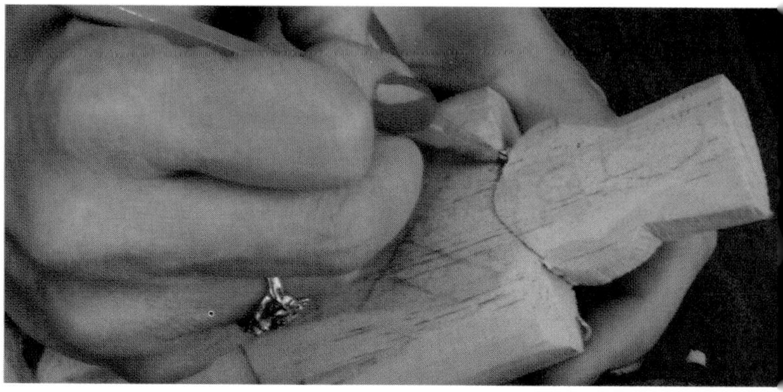

Redraw the chin...

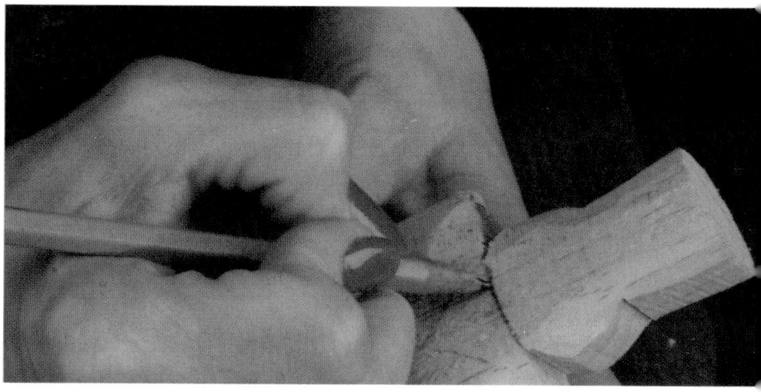

and the back of the head.

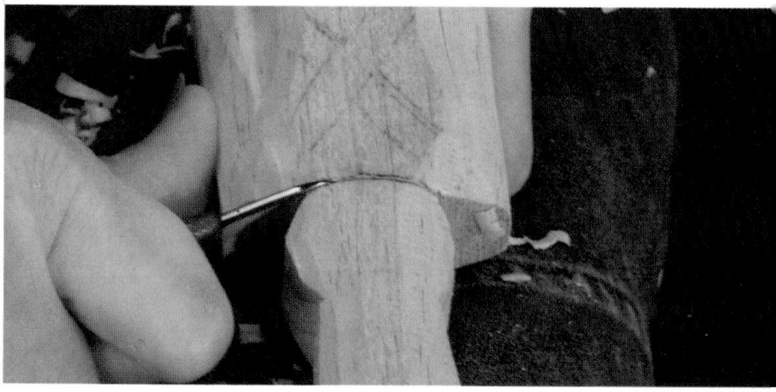

Score front and back...

and trim back to the line from the upper body.

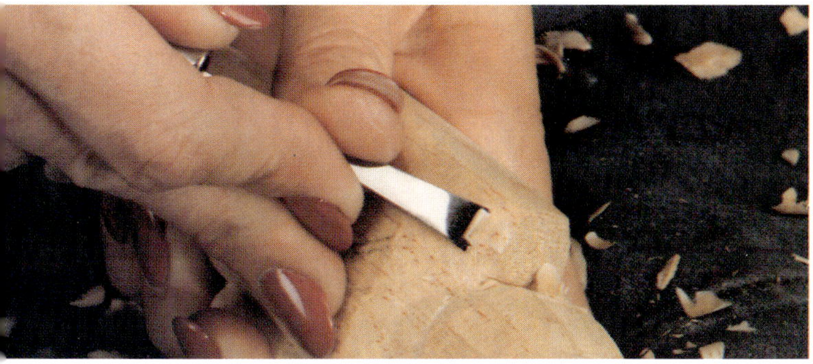

There are epaulets on the shoulders, so you want to be careful when shaping them.

Just skim off the saw marks from the tops of the epaulets.

I'm going to put details on the hat and head before working on the body. Begin by drawing in the line of the hat brim and visor.

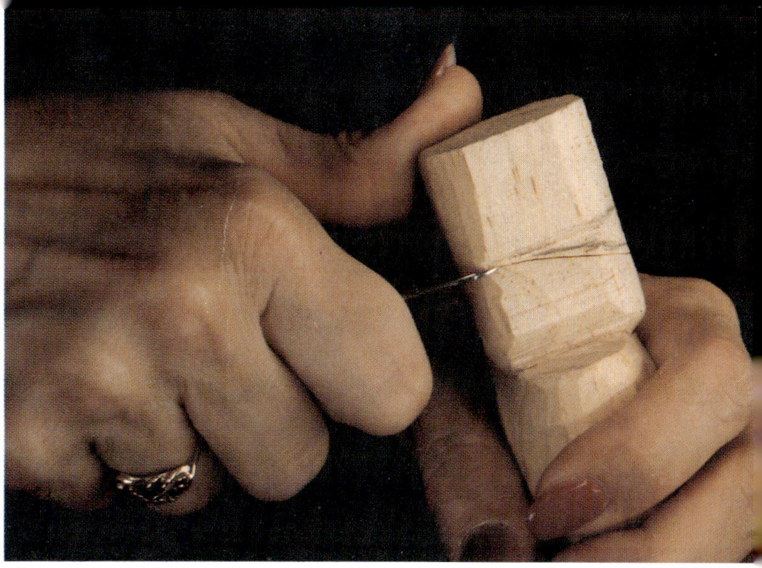

Score the line.

Trim back to it from the head.

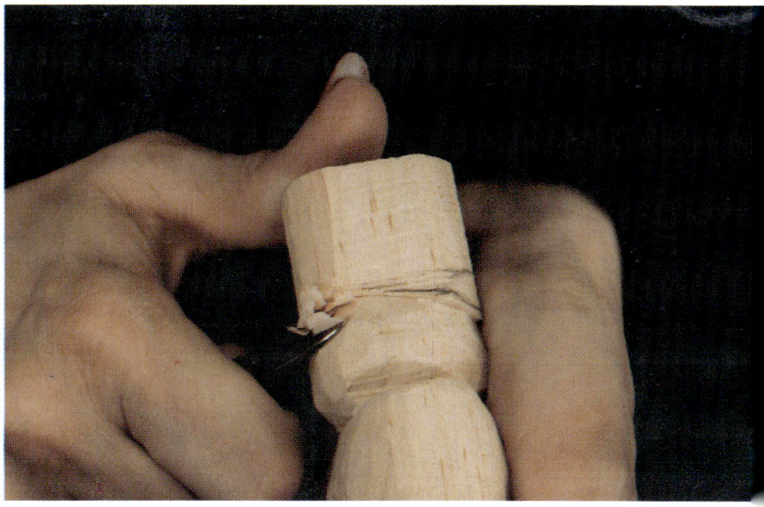

Deepen the score line at the back of the head and reduce the head back to it. This will allow me to shape the hat, giving it more of a flare.

Angle the back of the hat in a little bit.

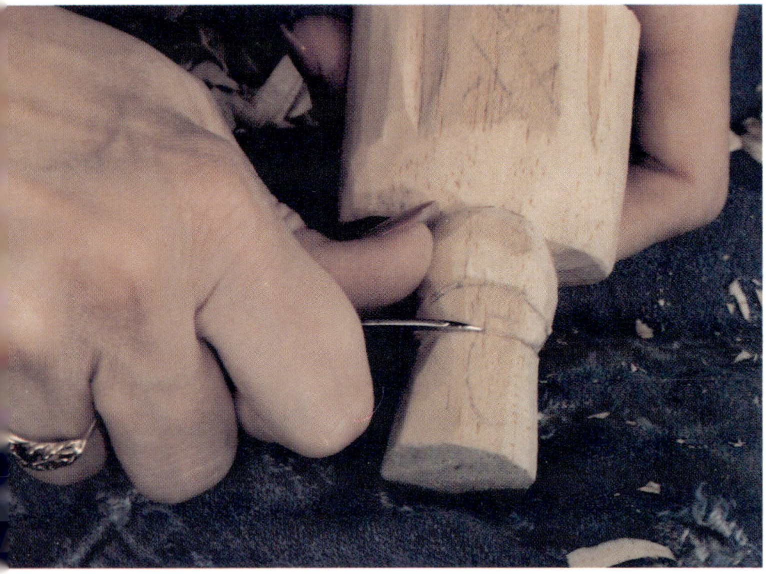

Score the line at the top of the visor.

Taper back to it from the crown...

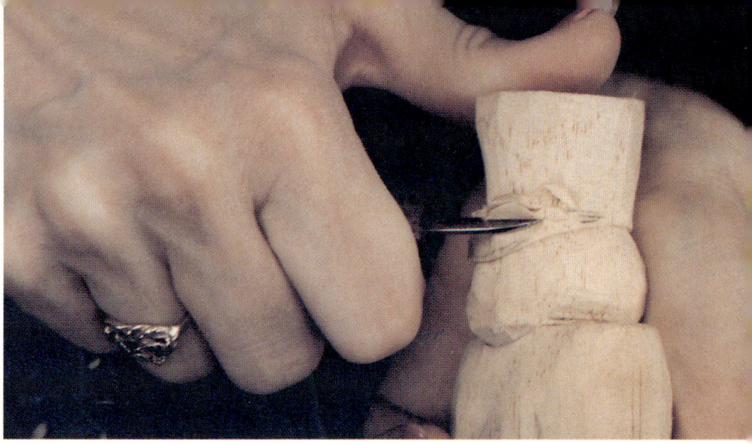

and the visor.

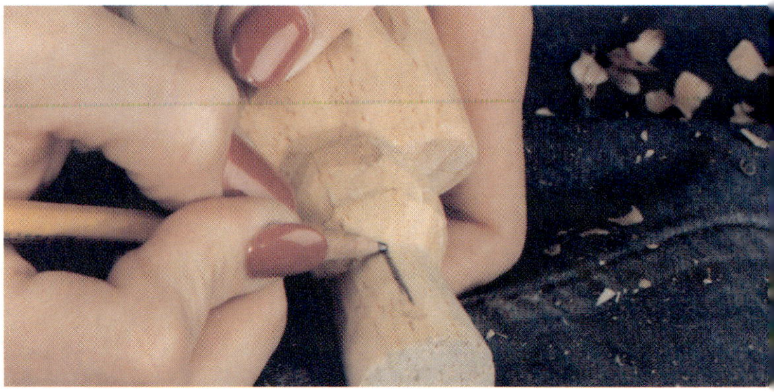

Draw the plume by making a line straight up the center...

with a small arc at the top.

Connect the ends of the arc with the bottom of the line.

Score the outline of the plume.

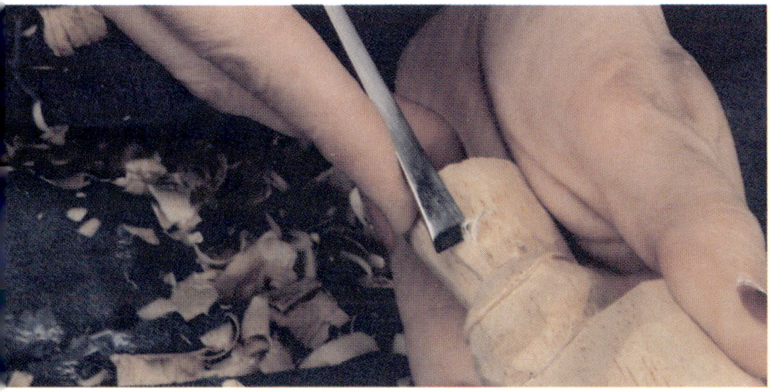

Round the plume with a chisel.

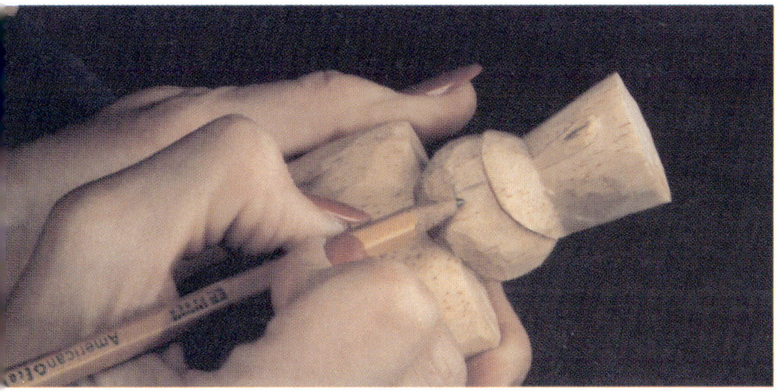

Draw the midline of the face and the bottom of the nose.

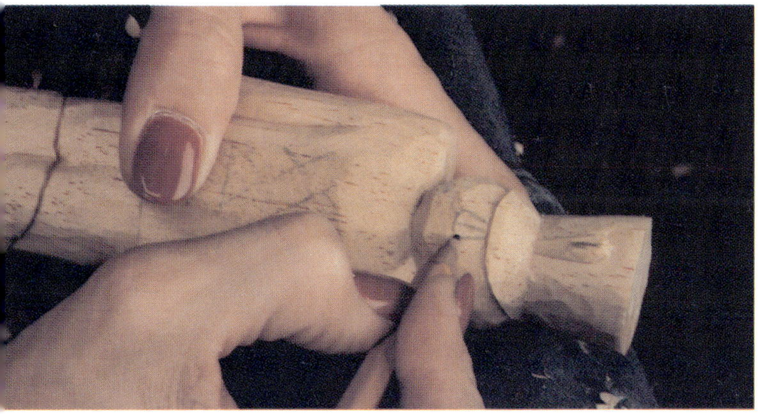

Finish drawing the nose.

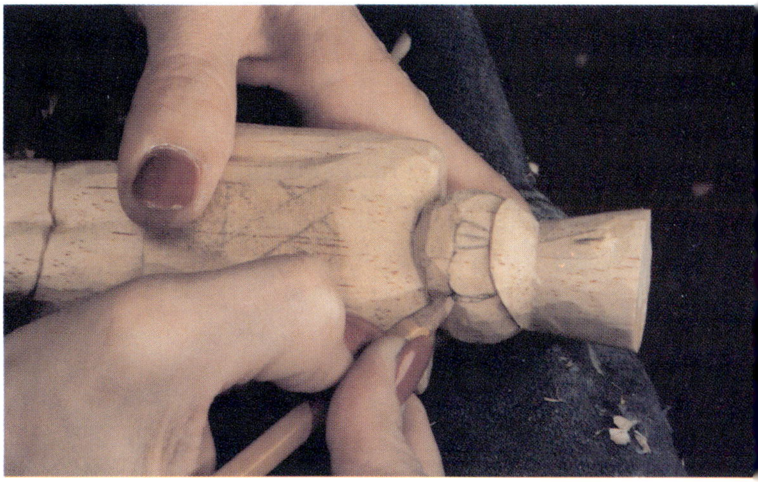

Draw the top of the moustache and carry the line up the sides of the cheeks.

Follow the center line down and draw an upside down v to set the bottom center of the moustache.

Finish drawing the bottom of the moustache and the front corners of the hairline.

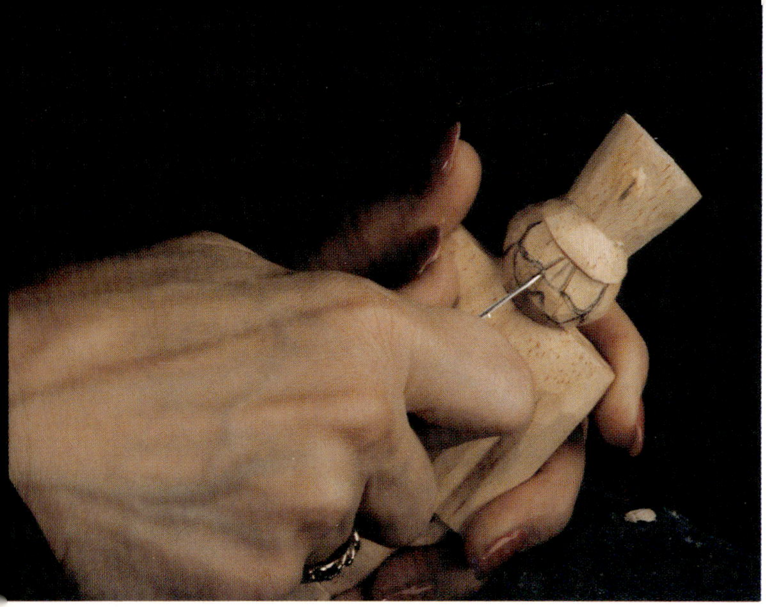

Score the sides of the nose, carrying the cut into the moustache.

Trim off the shavings beneath the visor.

Starting at the bottom of the moustache line...

Score the bottom of the nose...

follow the line of the nose and relieve the cheek area.

and trim the moustache back to it.

With the chisel at an angle, establish the planes of the nose.

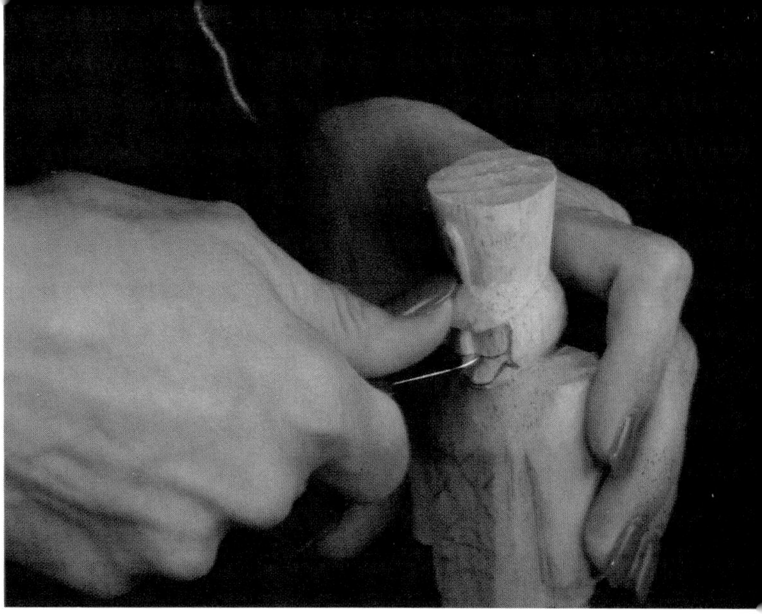

Score down the edge of the sideburns and across the top of the moustache.

Round the end of the nose.

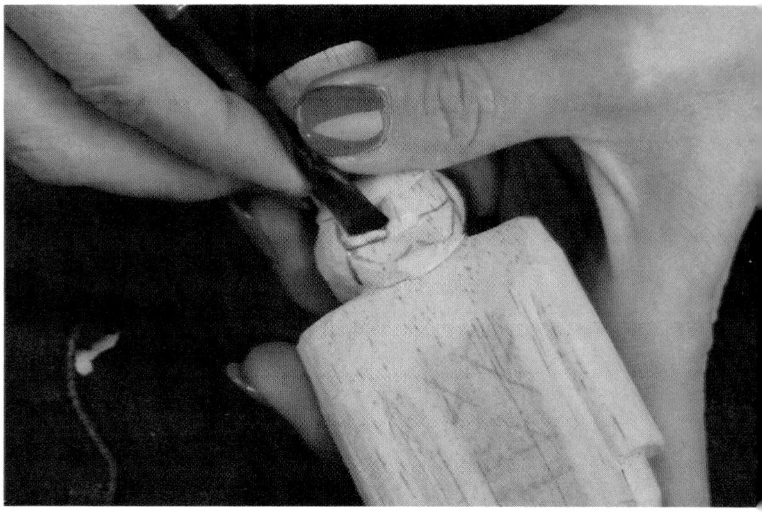

Carve back to the scored line from the cheek. This drops the cheek back.

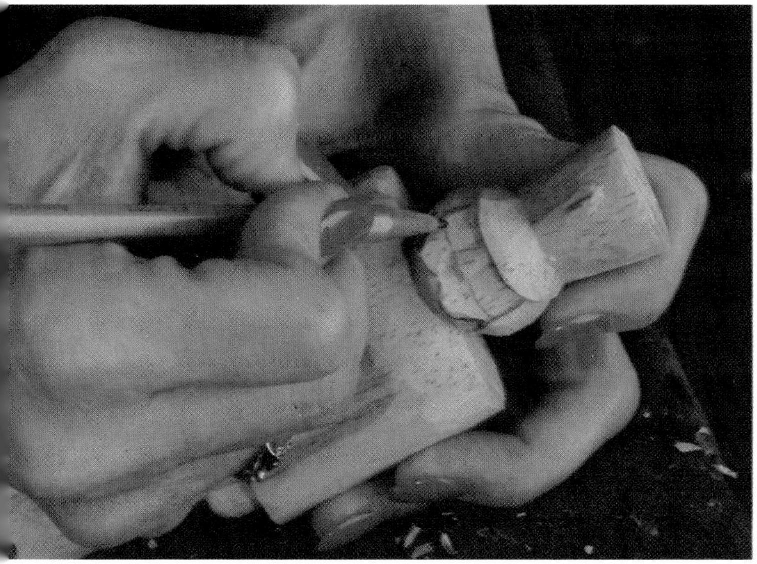

Redraw the moustache line.

The moustache is a little too thick, so I'll narrow to about here.

Score the bottom of the moustache...

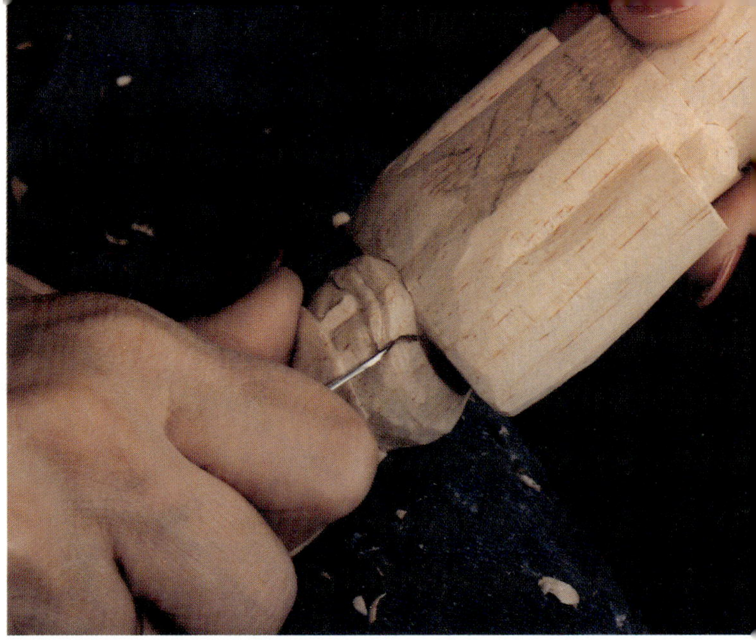

Score the side of the hair...

and trim back to it from the chin.

and shape the chin.

Round over the moustache.

The face is established...

and the head completed.

Trim back to it from the bottom of the coat...

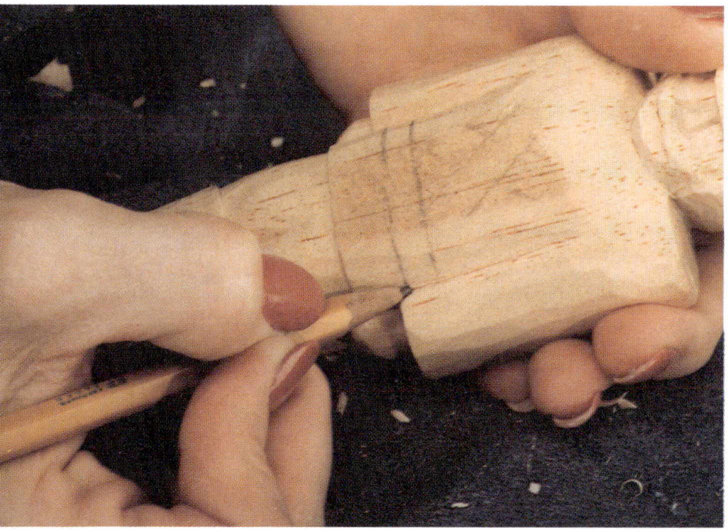

Redraw the belt. The criss-cross straps are just painted.

and the top.

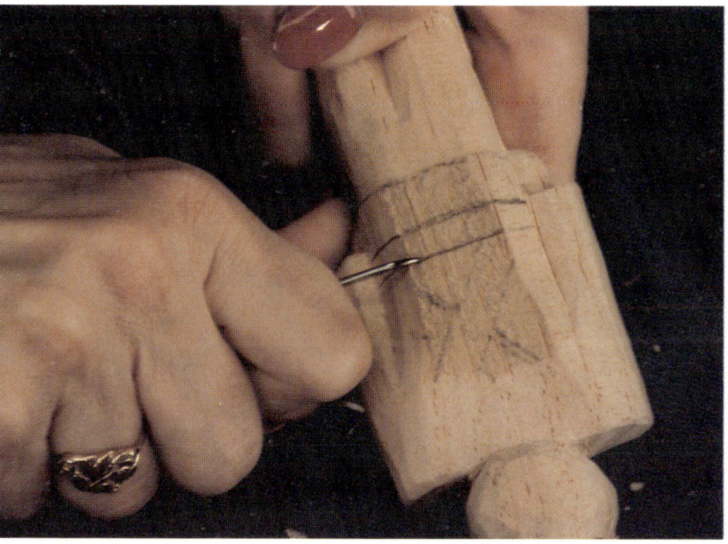

Score the lines of the belt, top and bottom, front and back.

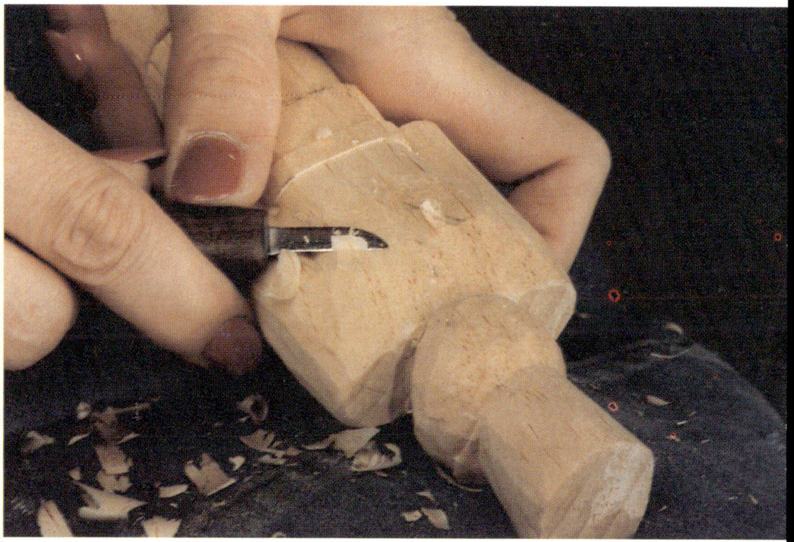

Clean up the upper body.

Draw in the epaulets...

and around the fringe.

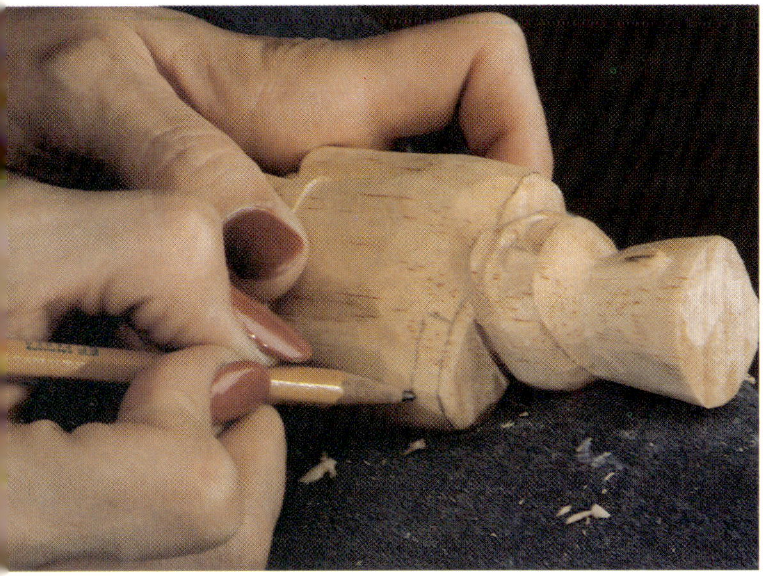

and their fringes.

Carve the shoulders up underneath the fringe.

Run the V-tool along the lower edge of the epaulets...

Use the v-tool to create the strands of the fringe.

Ready for painting.

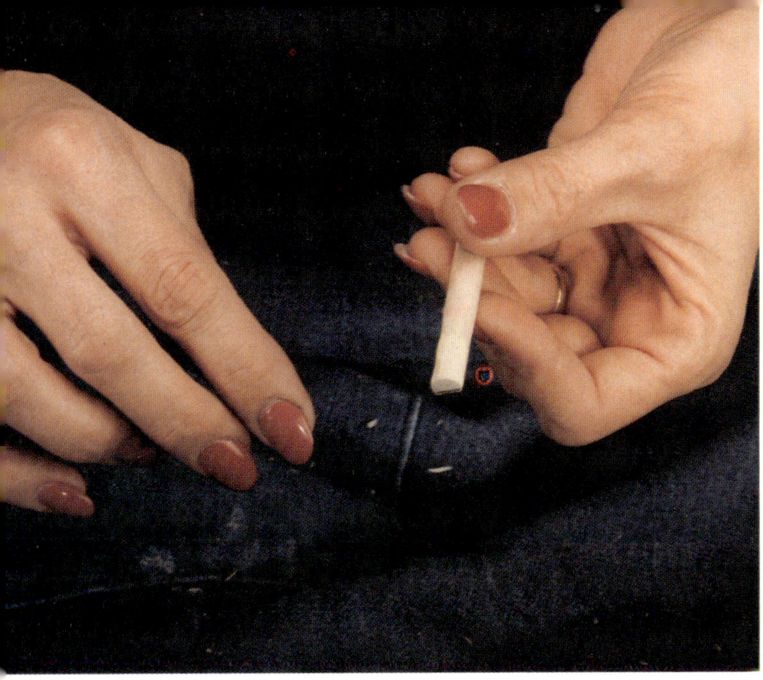

Apply glue to the rounded area of the dowels, being careful not to get any on the flat section. This would interrupt the flow of air.

Insert the dowels.

Test and adjust so both chambers whistle. Set aside and let the glue set.

Carving the Santa Ornament

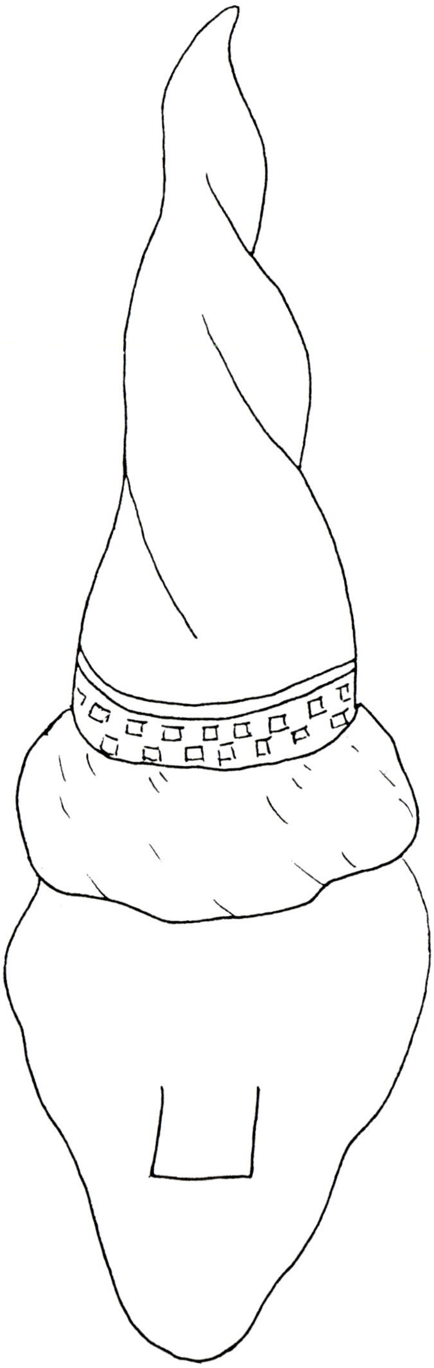

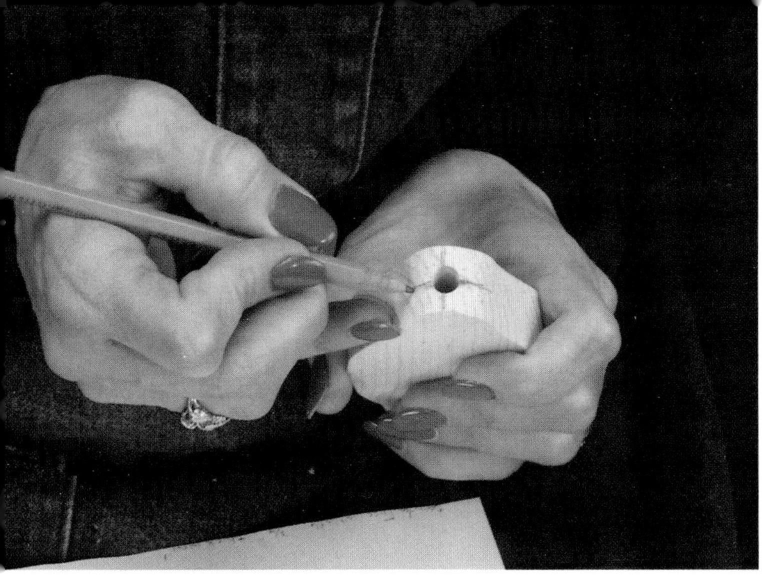

The hole in the Santa whistle is centered in the bottom. It is easiest to drill this before cutting out the pattern while the stock is still square. The wood is 3/4" thick.

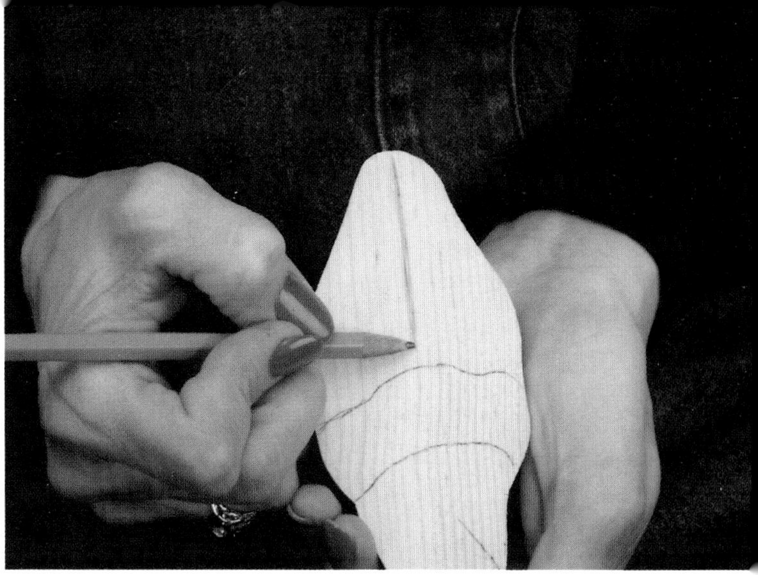

Unlike the soldier, there is no natural angle for the placement of the reed, so I'll put it on the back. Turn the piece over and draw a line that indicates the position of the air hole.

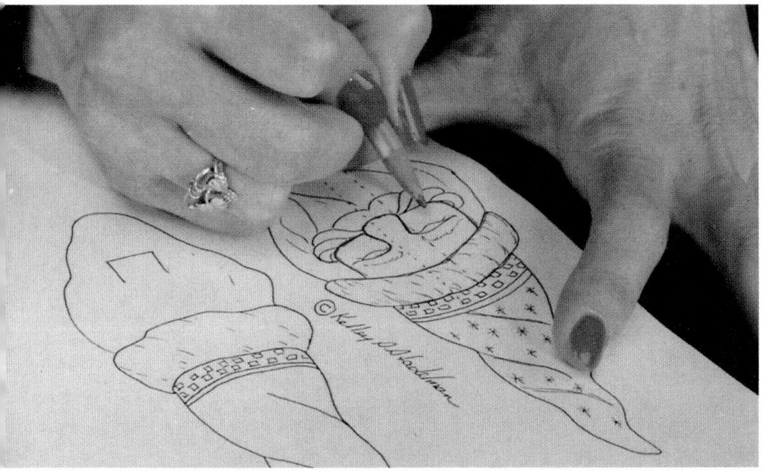

After drilling the hole and cutting the blank, transfer the facial features to the blank.

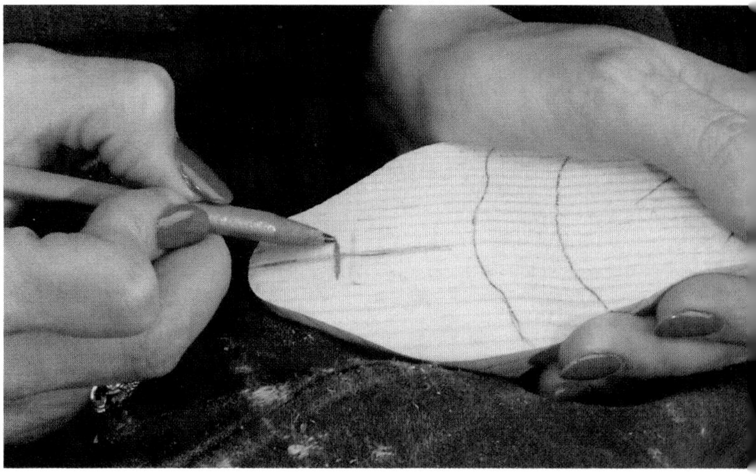

The straight cut for the whistle will be about one inch from the bottom.

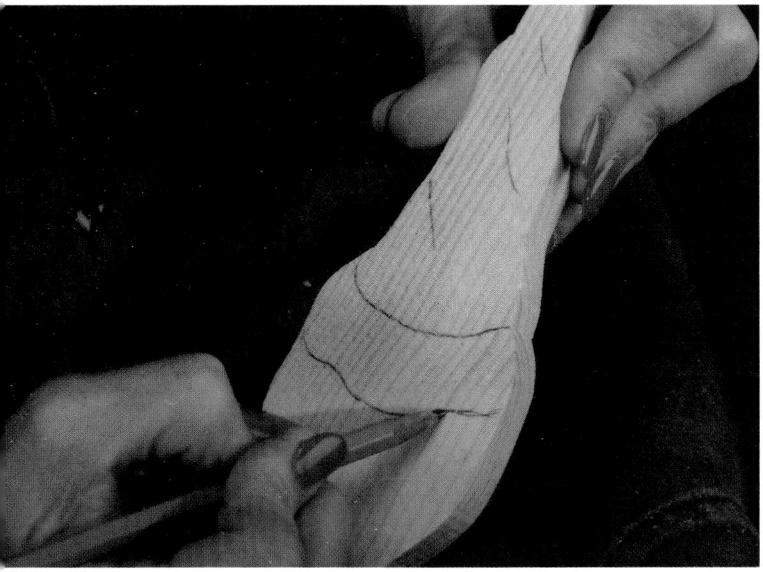

Draw the fur lines in the back.

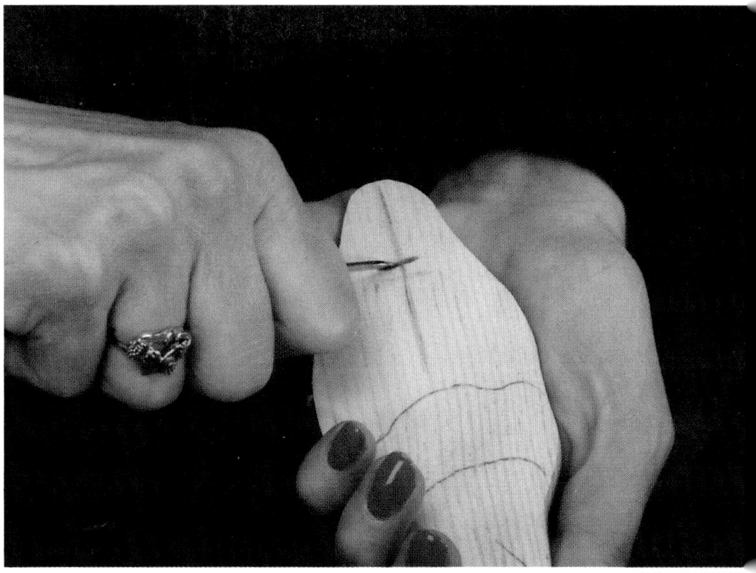

Score that line...

and cut a wedge back to it from above.

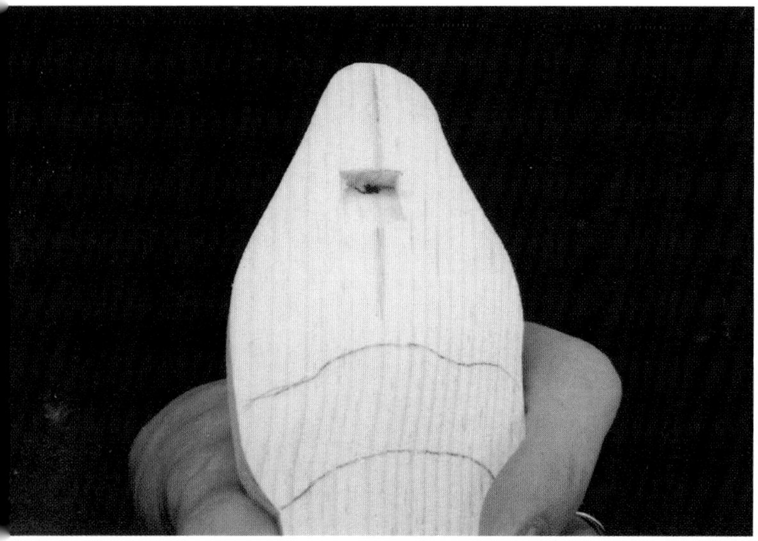

Repeat the process until about one half of the drilled hole is exposed.

Mark the end of a dowel about 1/3 of the way down.

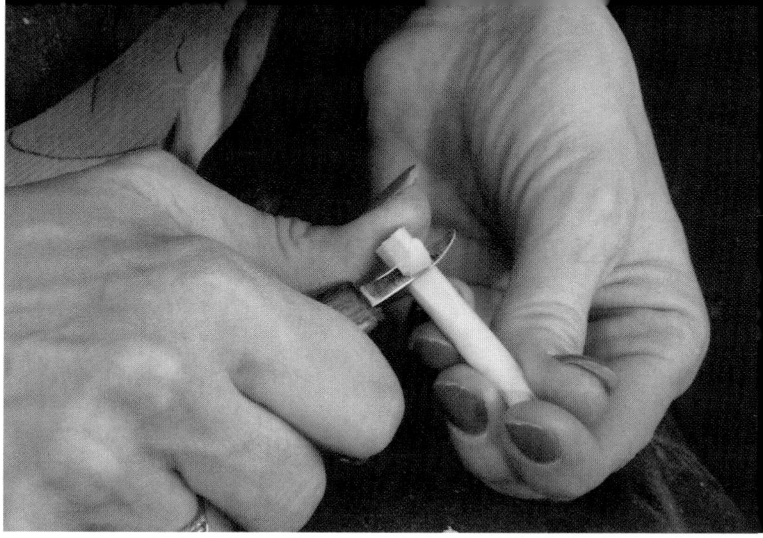

Flatten one side down to the line.

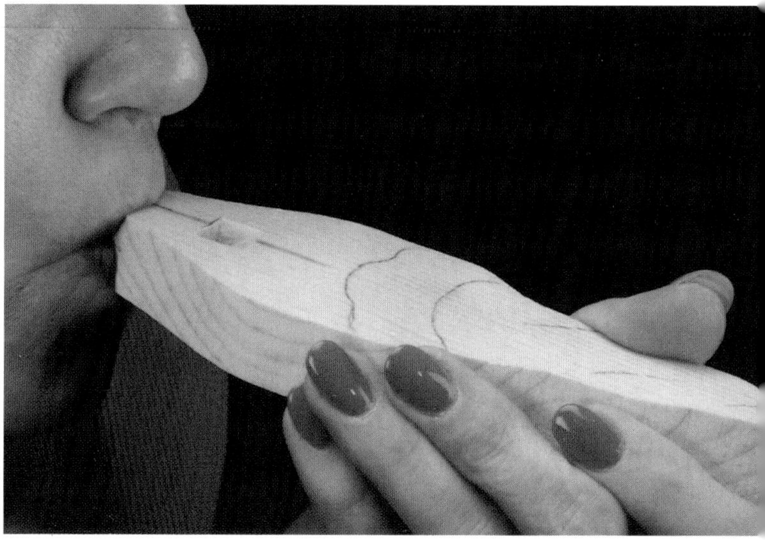

Slide the dowel into the hole until its end is flush with the straight edge of the opening. Test it for a whistle. If it doesn't work try pushing the dowel in a little further.

If it still doesn't work, drop the angle of the reed down just a little. Do this in small steps until the whistle works.

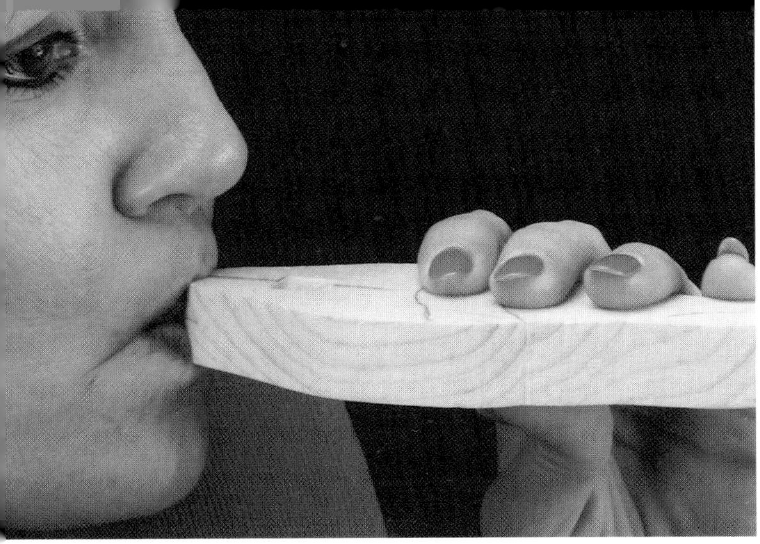

Test it again.

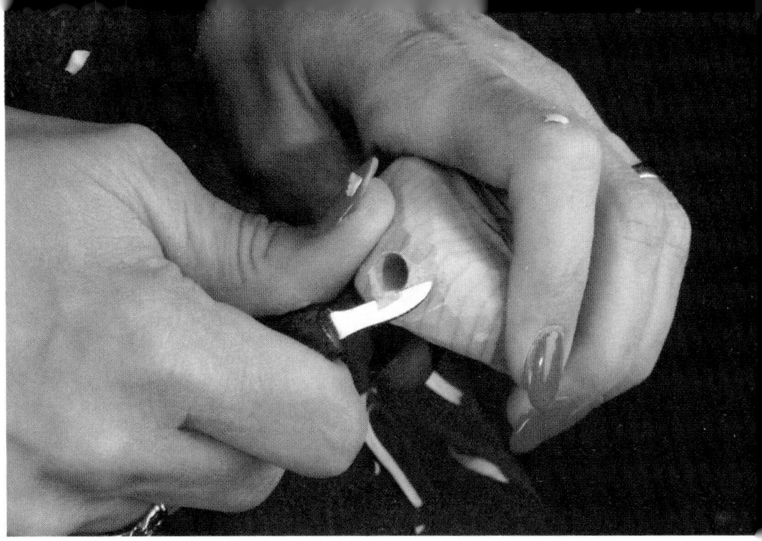

Shape around the blow hole.

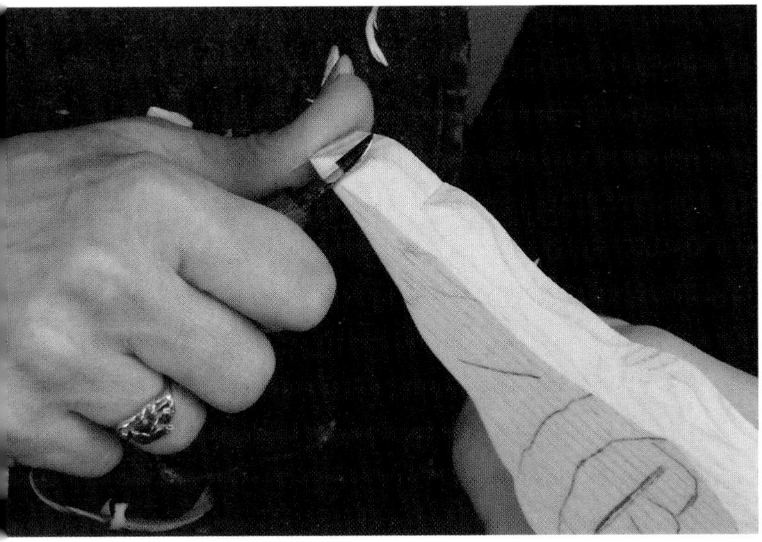

When it whistles, remove the dowel and begin carving. Start by rounding down the edges all around.

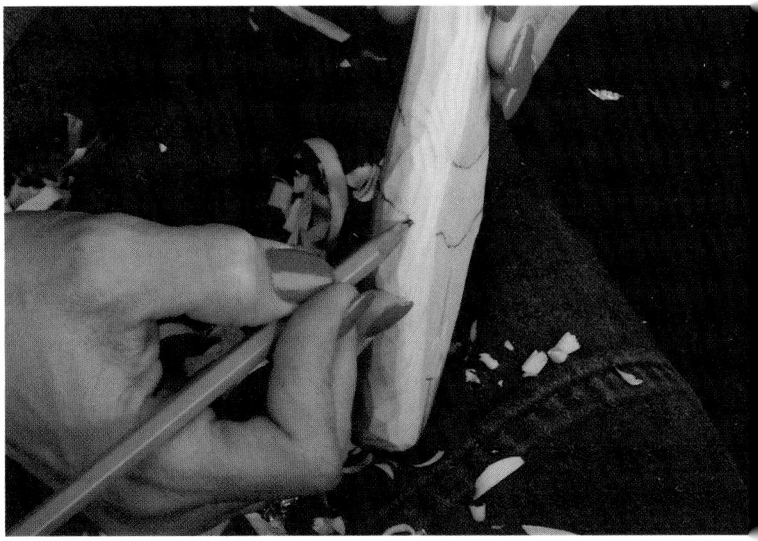

When the edges are rounded join the front and back patterns.

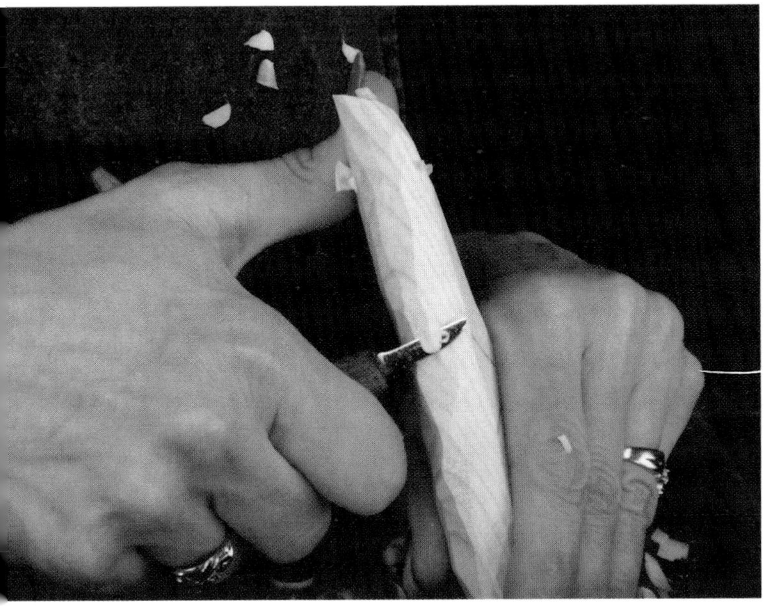

Take the top of the hat to a point.

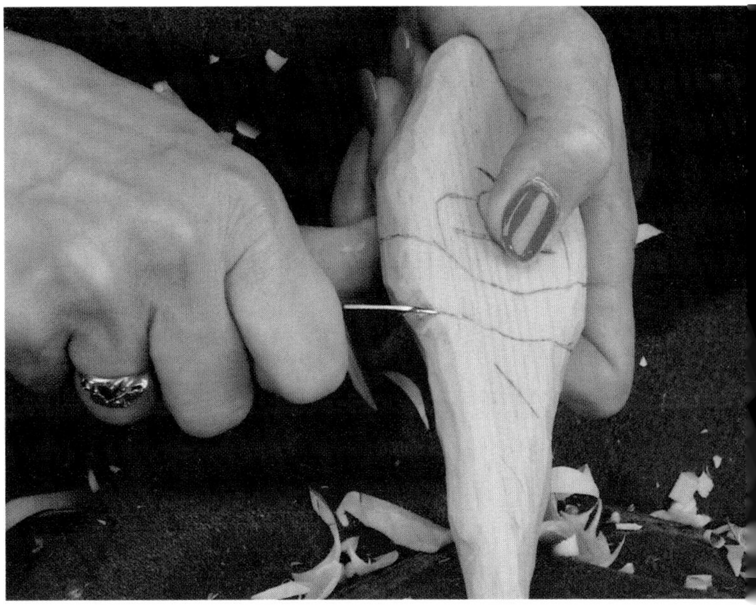

Score the fur top and bottom, all the way around.

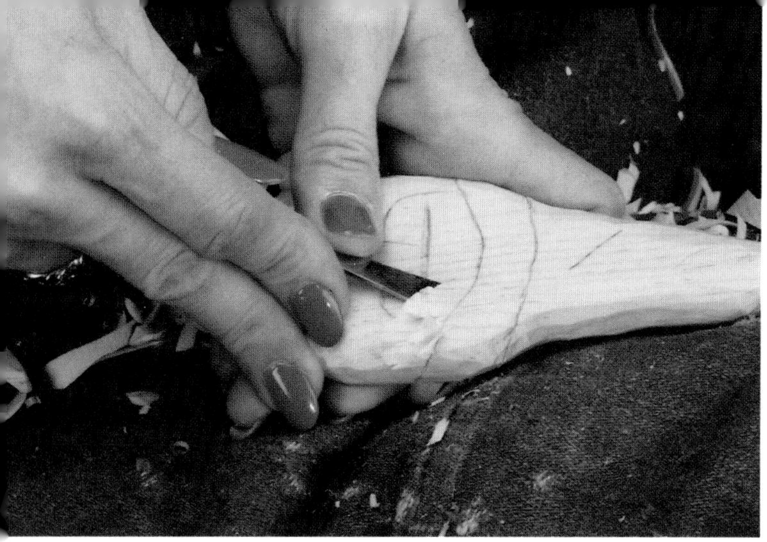

Chisel back to the bottom line of the cap from the face and hair...

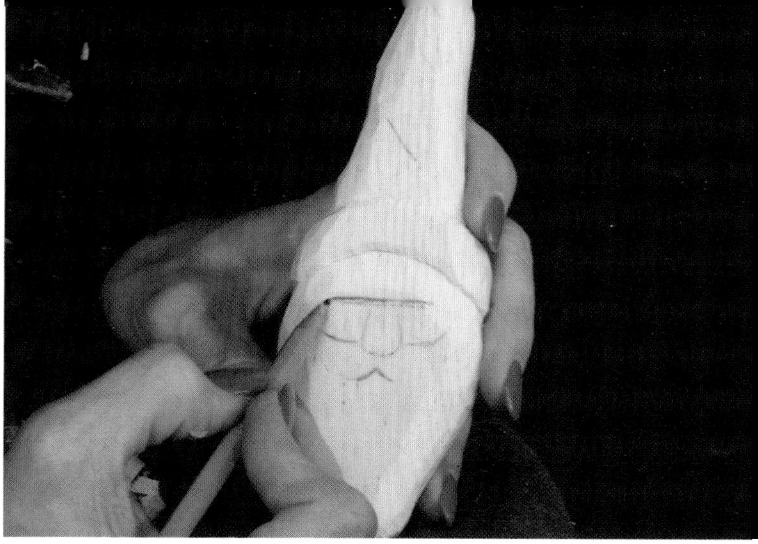

Draw a line straight across for the eyes...

and to the top line from the crown. A knife will clean up the chips. Be careful not to go too deeply or you will hit the hole.

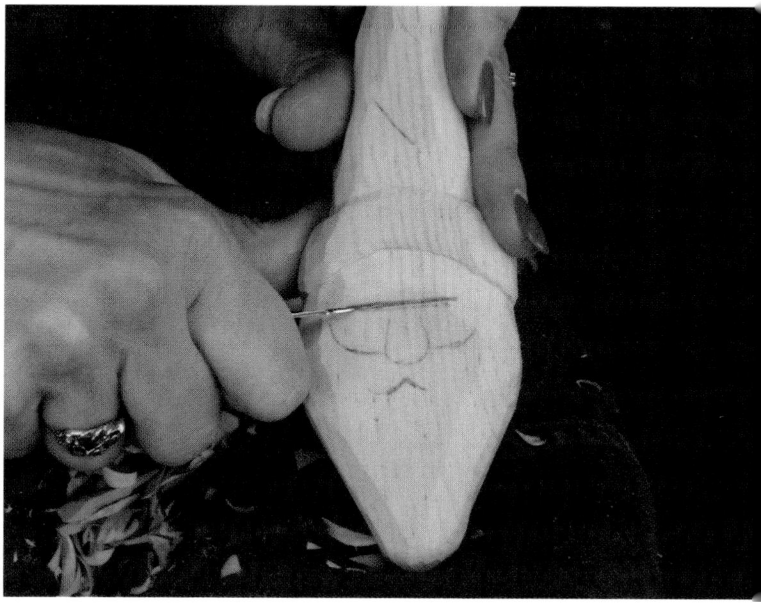

and score it.

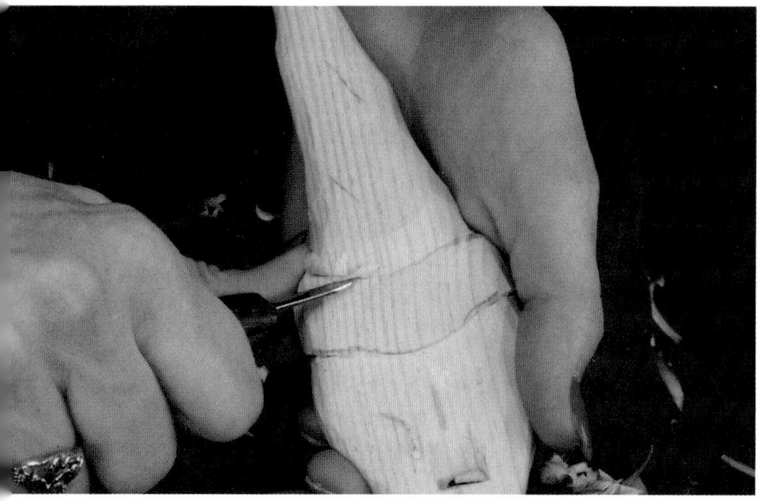

Round off the edge of the fur.

From just above that line come back with a wedge cut, using a chisel.

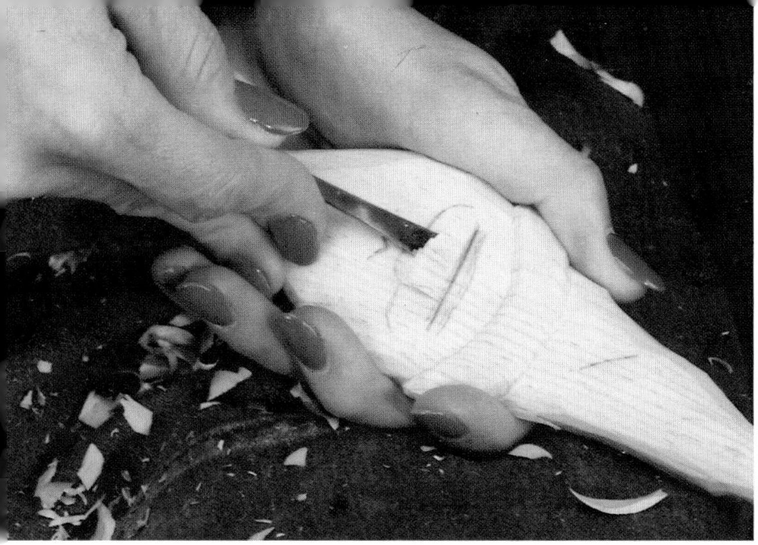

Go to the side of the nose and make a wedge cut up to the same line.

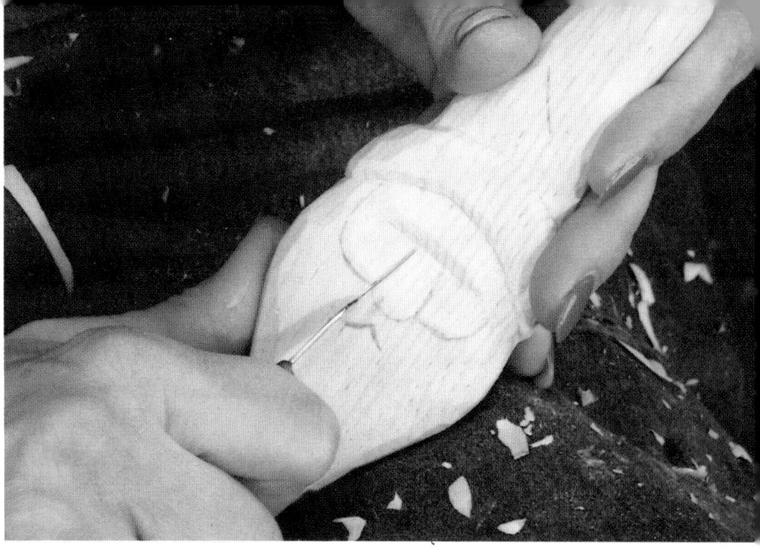

and score them past the end of the nose.

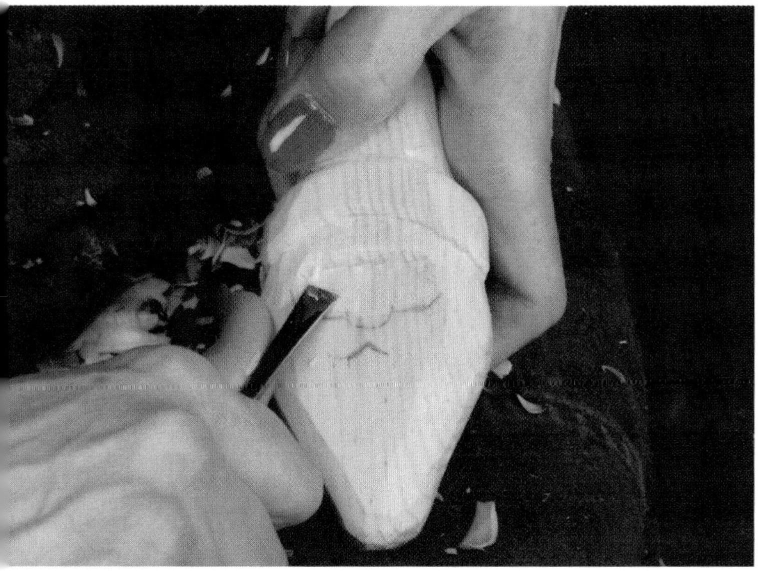

Repeat until you get enough depth. This establishes the slope of the nose and the recess of the eyes.

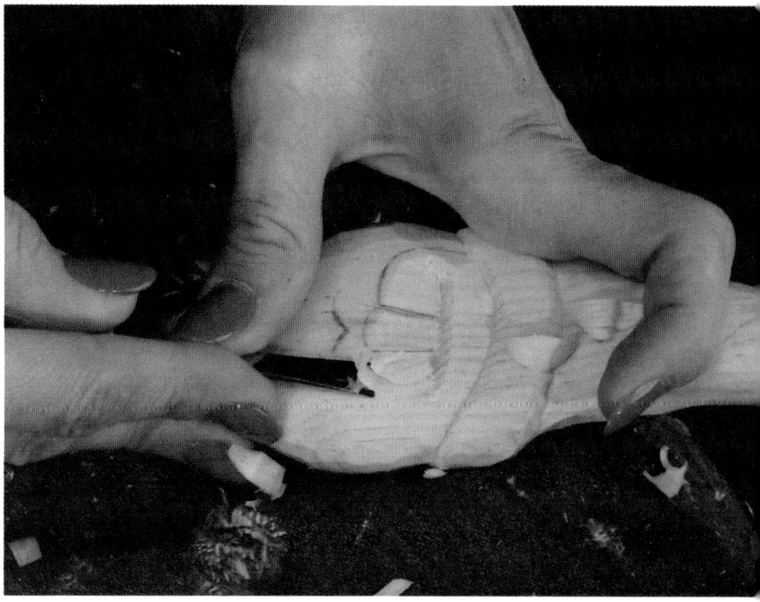

Come up beside the nose to drop the cheeks back.

Redraw the lines of the nose...

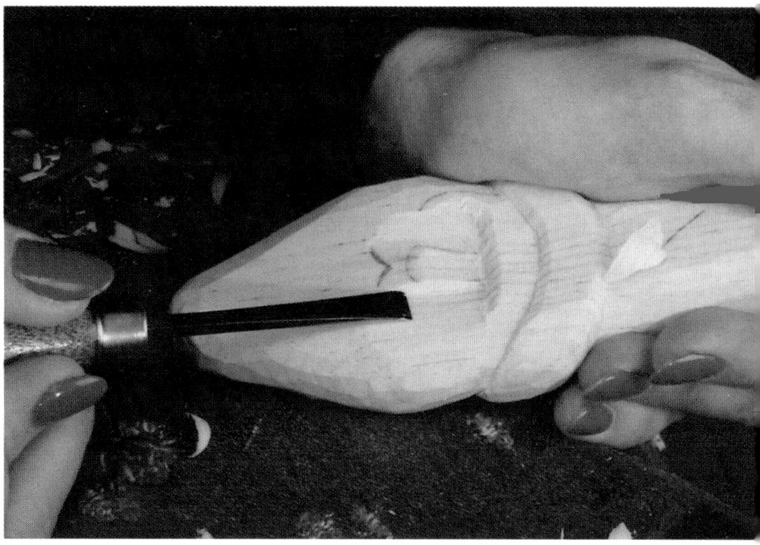

The deepest part of the cheek cut needs to be at the end of the nose so it stands out. The cut should taper at the eye.

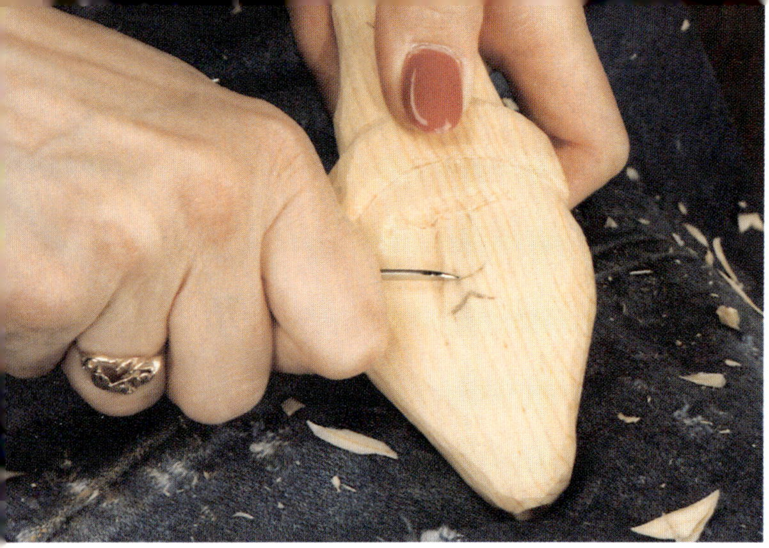

Score the bottom of the nose.

Round off the end of the nose.

Wedge back to the nose from the moustache.

Redraw the center line of the nose and shape the sides so the highest point runs down the middle.

Progress.

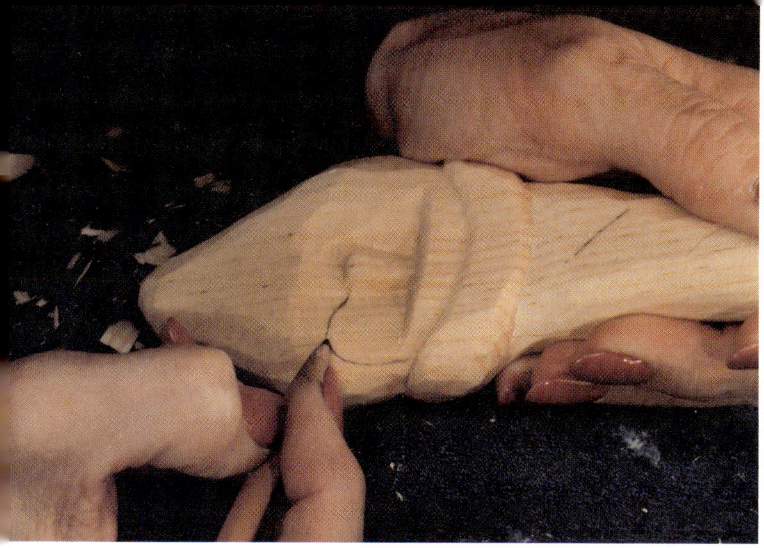

Redraw the top of the moustache and the cheek lines.

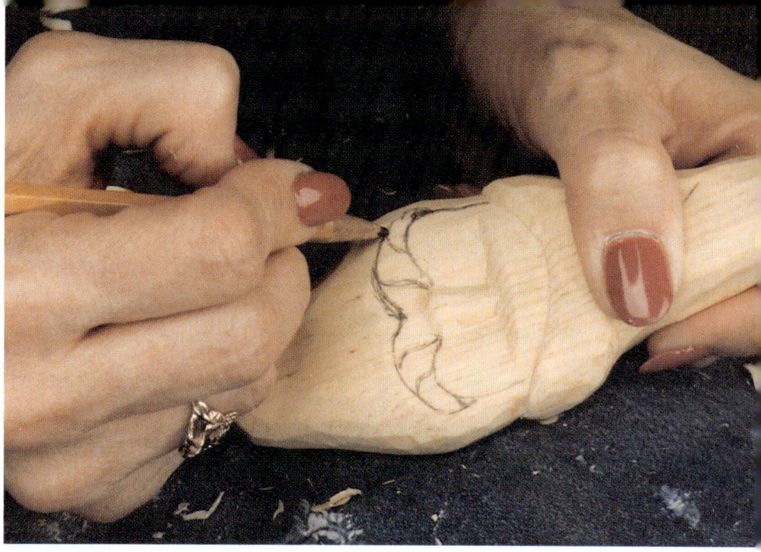

Refer to the pattern and draw in the major segments of the moustache.

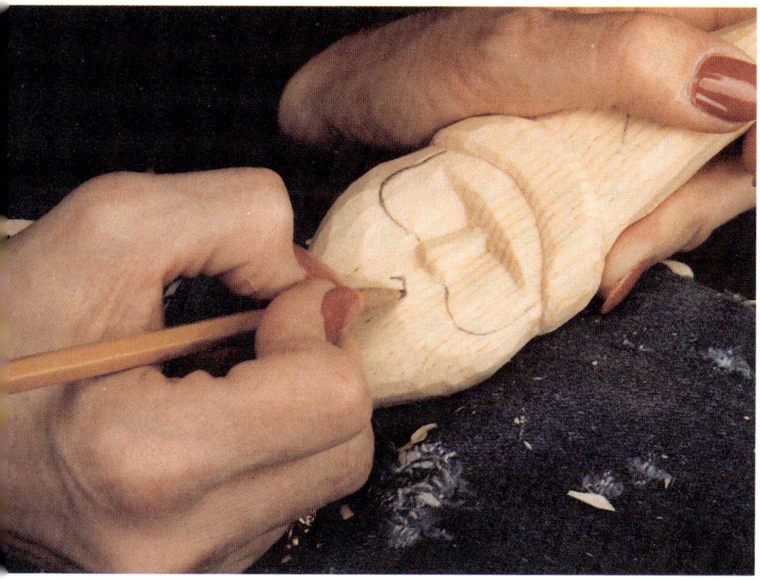

With an upside down vee, set the center of the lower edge of the moustache...

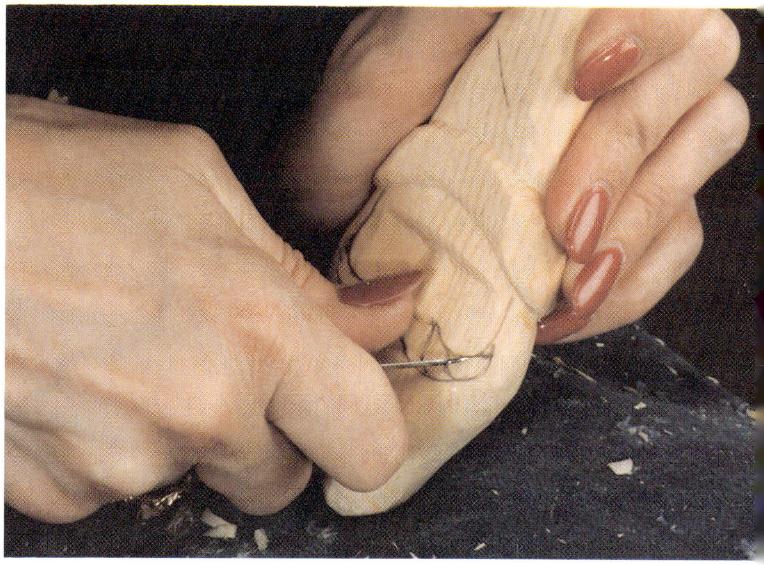

Score around the cheek line and the top of the moustache to the sides of the nose.

and draw it in.

Cut back to the score line from the cheek.

Round the hair and the top of the moustache back to the cheek.

Progress.

Drop the brow down in the middle, giving it a separation above the bridge of the nose.

Drawing a line in the crease will help you see if the eyes are straight across. The figure's right eye goes up a little so I need to drop it down.

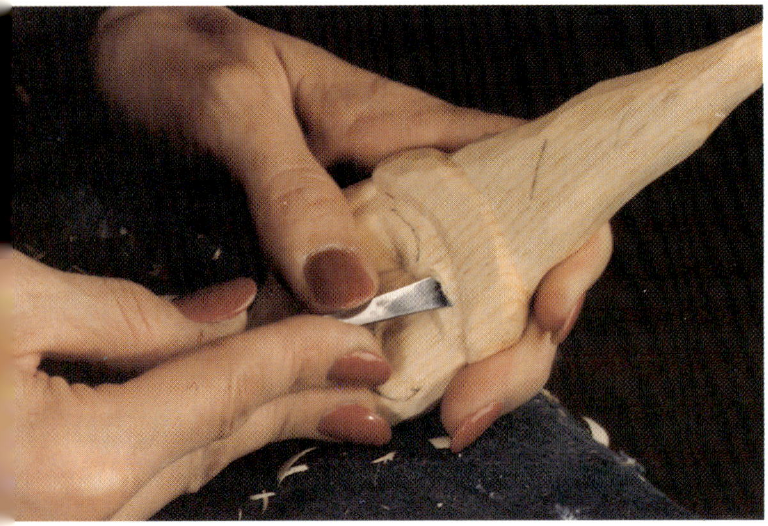

Draw in the tops of the eyebrows. Start there and scoop the forehead back to the hat.

If it needs to go down I carve down from the top...

and clip the chip from the bottom. Do the opposite if the eye is going down a little.

Trim back to the line from below.

To create the eye, score a line that arches slightly over the center line.

The result. Do the other side in the same way.

At the end cut the line so it turns up.

Score the bottom edge of the moustache.

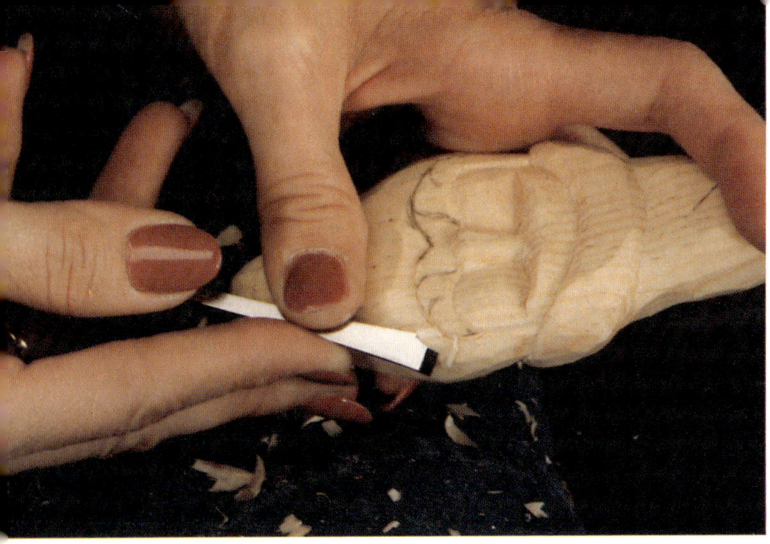

Trim back to it from the beard.

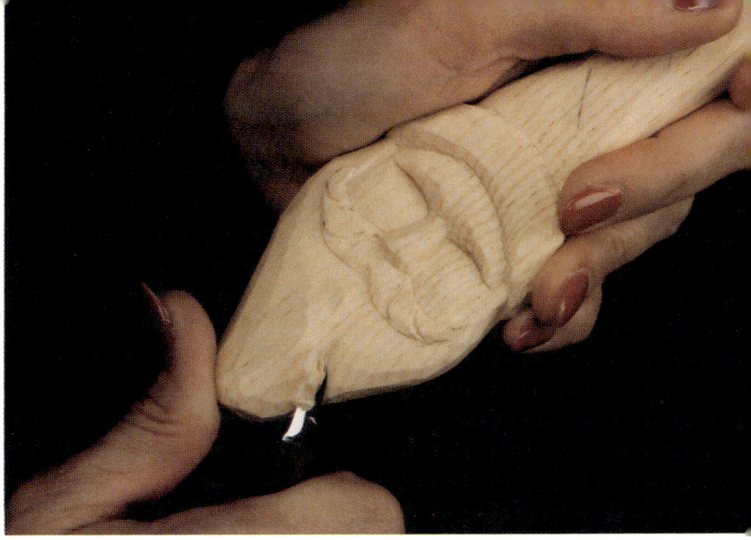

There is a bit of a swirl to the beard, so I need to scoop out some little valleys.

Round off the bottom of the moustache.

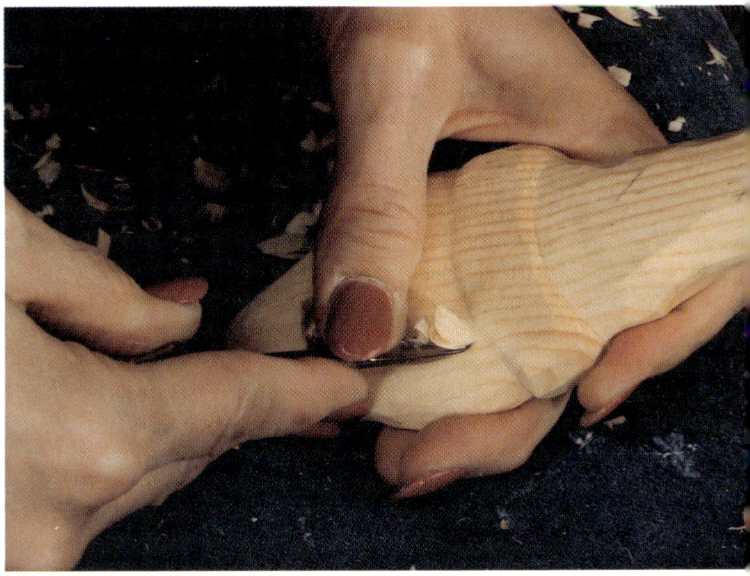

In the back I add some lower areas with a gouge to give the hair more interest.

On the segment lines, make some pretty deep grooves with a v-tool.

The hat is spiraled. Refer to the pattern and draw them in, continuing the spiral all around.

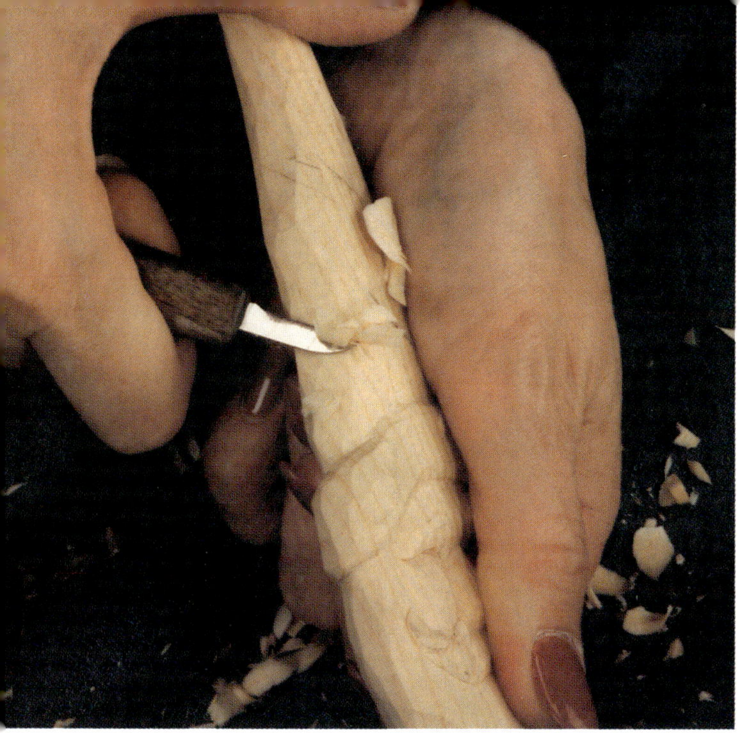

Scoop along the line to create the spiral.

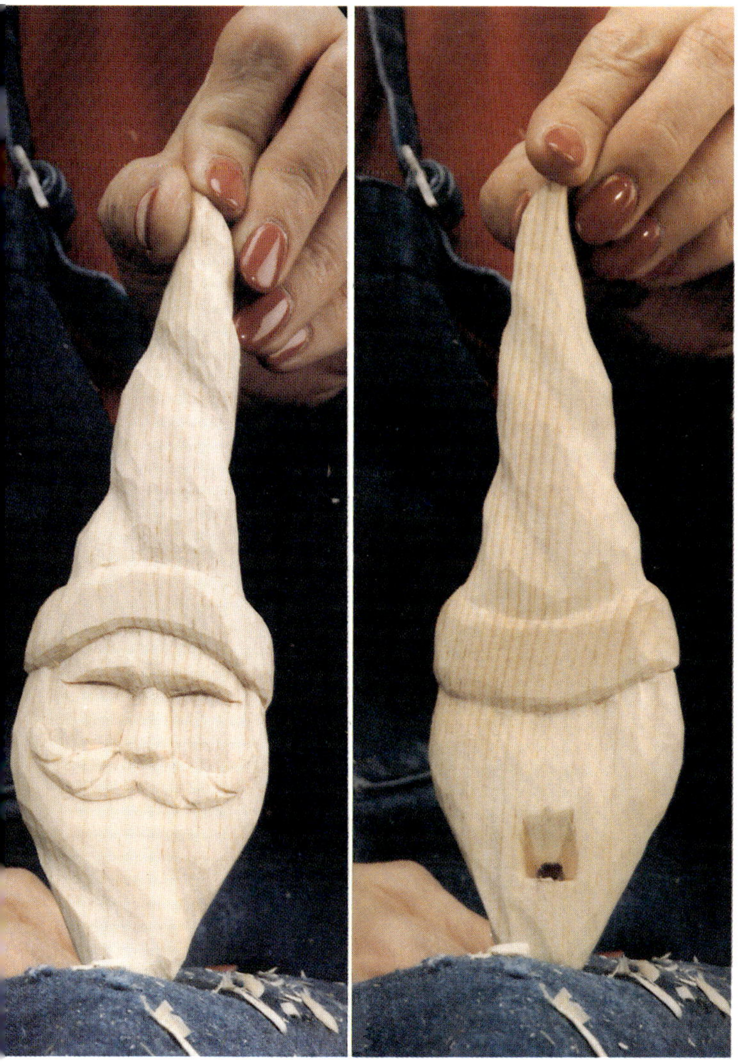

Ready for texturing.

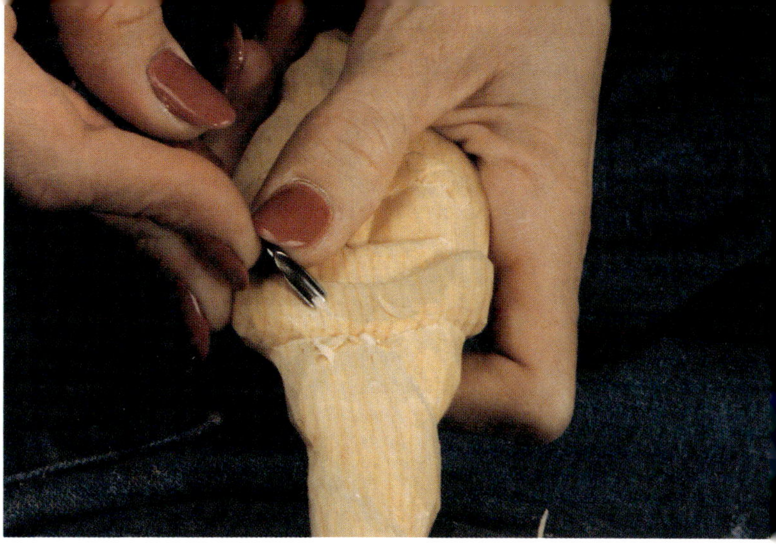

With a micro gouge, create the fur lines at a slight angle.

The result.

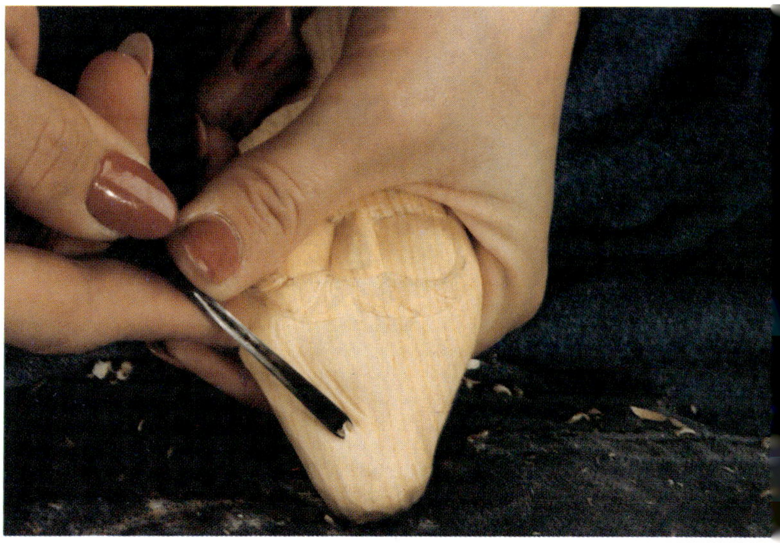

A v-tool creates the texture of the hair. Follow the swirl direction you established earlier.

Continue with the moustache in the same way.

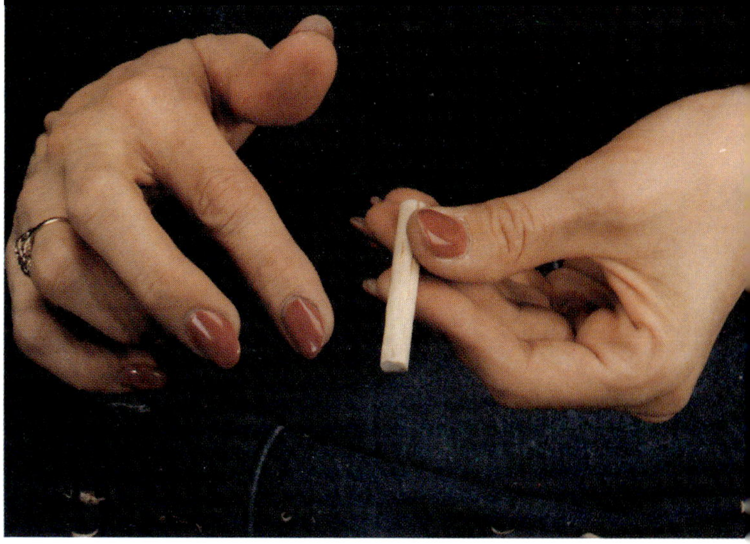

Apply a light coat of carpenter's glue to the round portion of the dowel, keeping the flat edge free of glue.

Insert the dowel in the whistle...

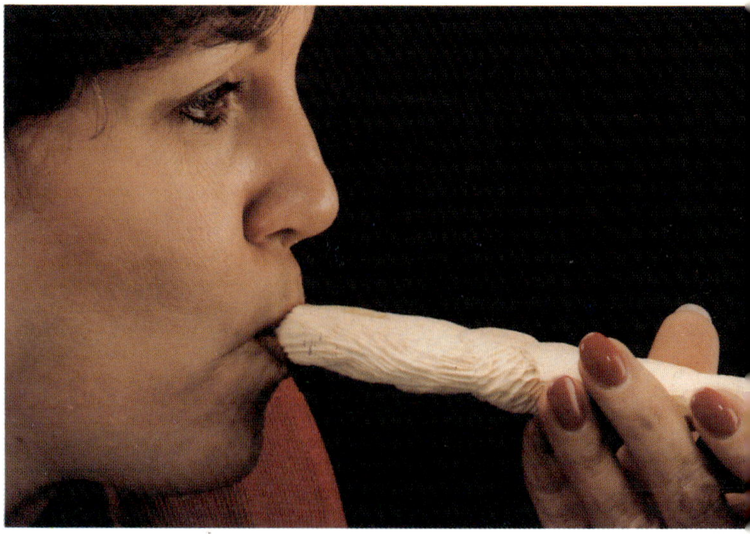

and test it. Adjust the dowel as necessary before the glue sets.

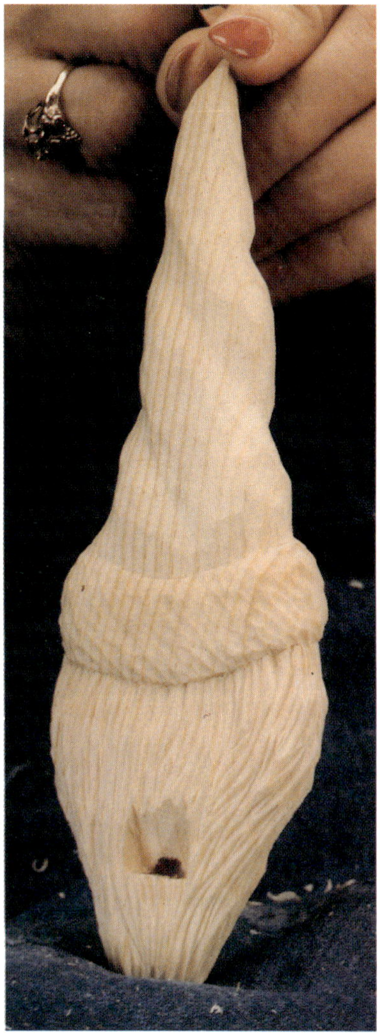

The carving complete.

Painting the Toy Soldier

Soldier Blue

Napthol Red Light

Warm Gold

Black

Peaches and Cream

Nutmeg

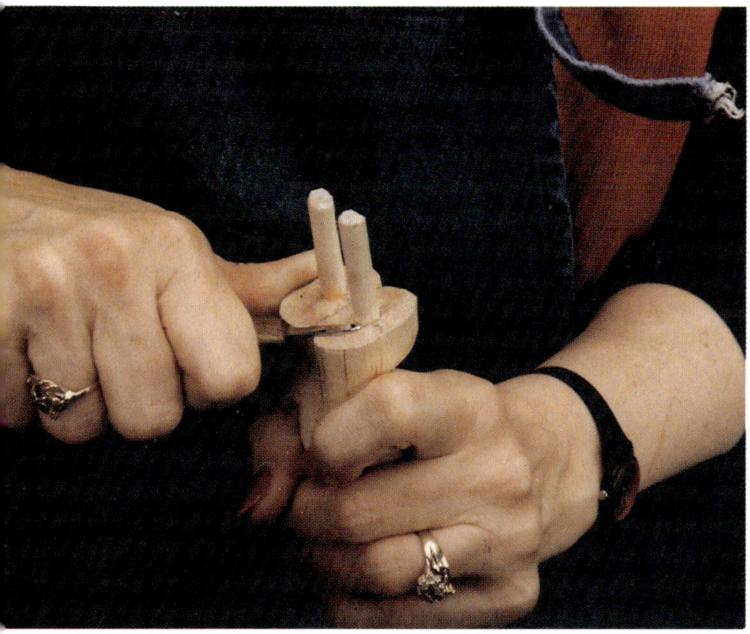

Before painting, carve the dowels...

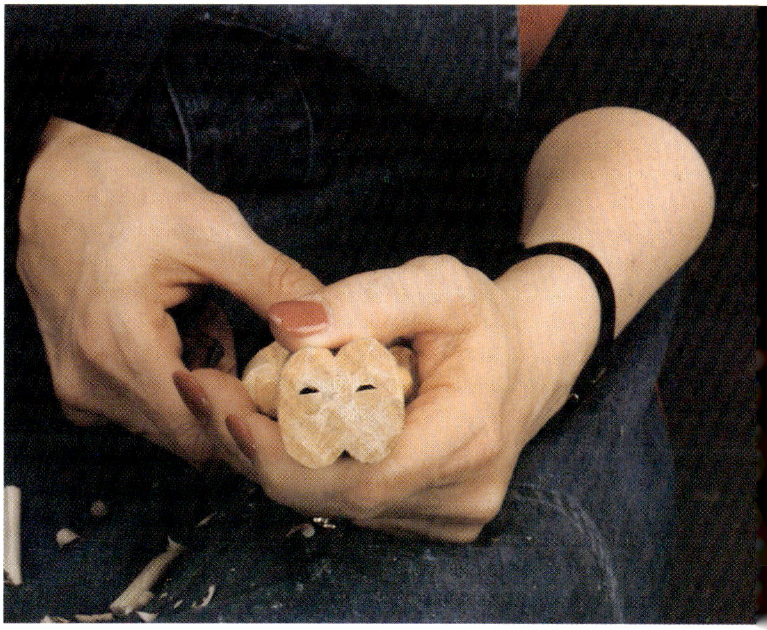

so they are flush with the bottom.

Paint the face with peaches and cream.

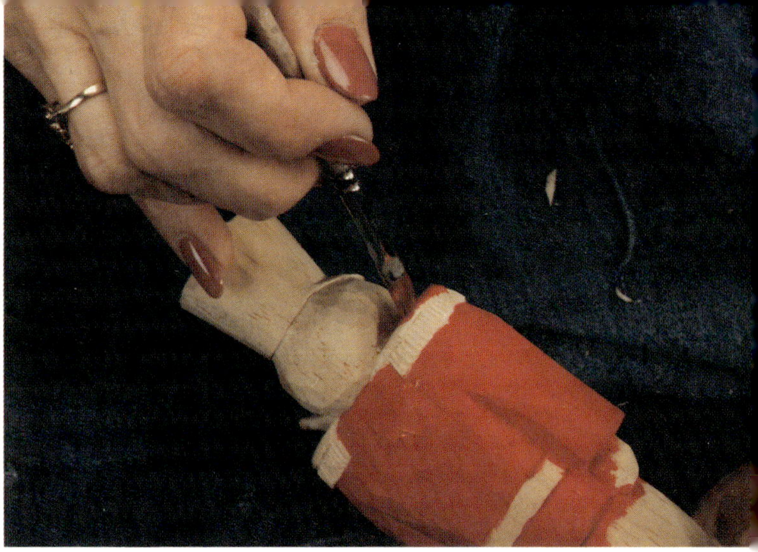

Paint the surface and edge of the epaulet in the same red.

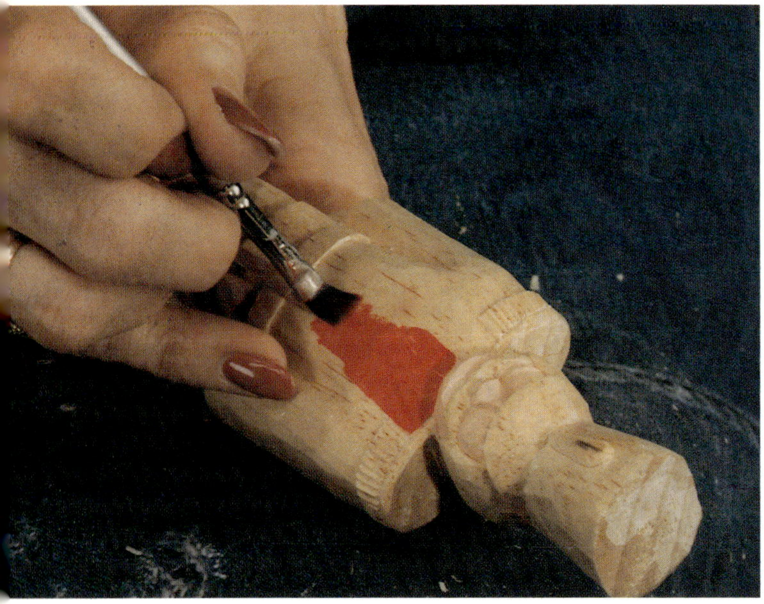

Paint the coat red.

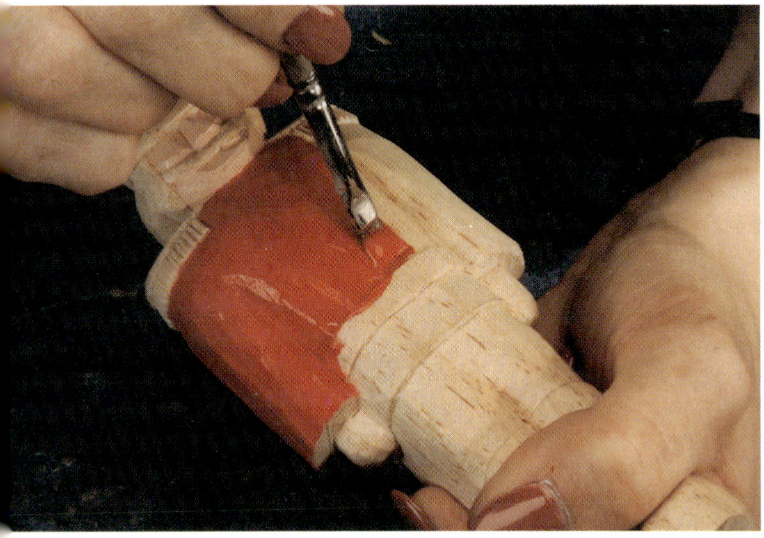

At the belt you don't need to be concerned about over painting. The black will cover the red in one coat.

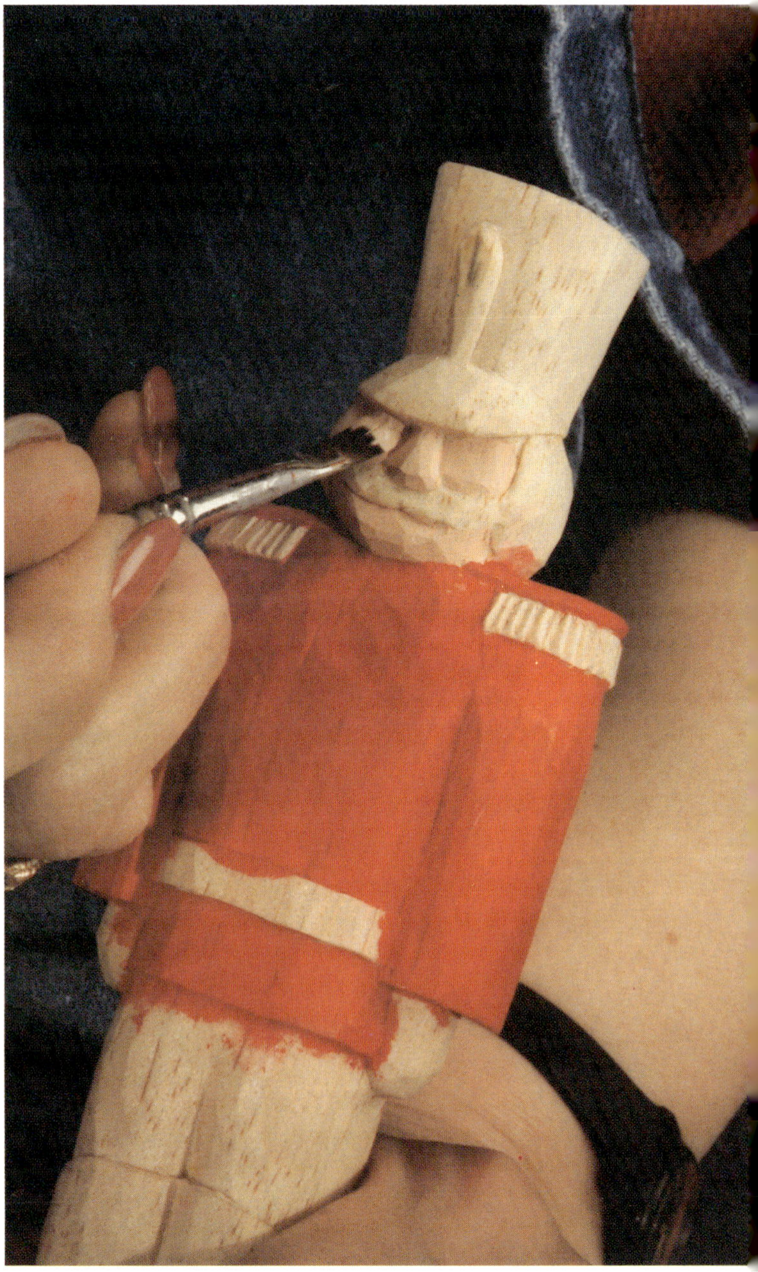

Apply a second coat of peaches and cream to the face.

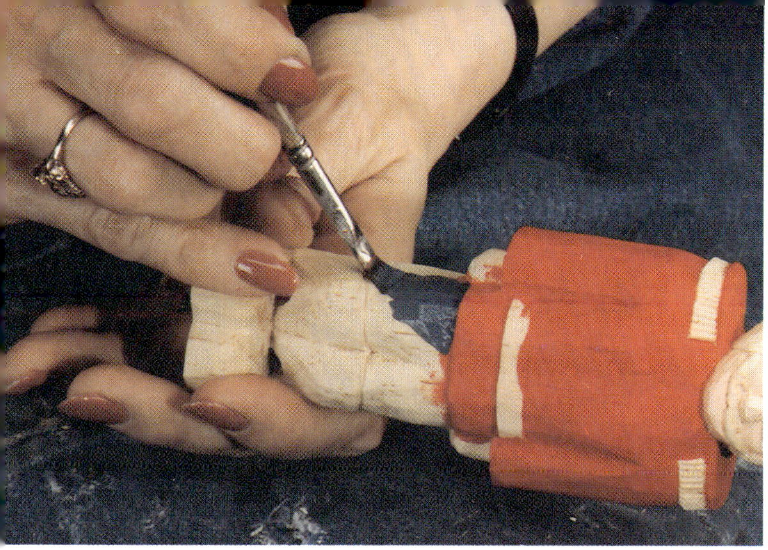

Paint the pants soldier blue.

the boots (don't let much paint go down the hole)...

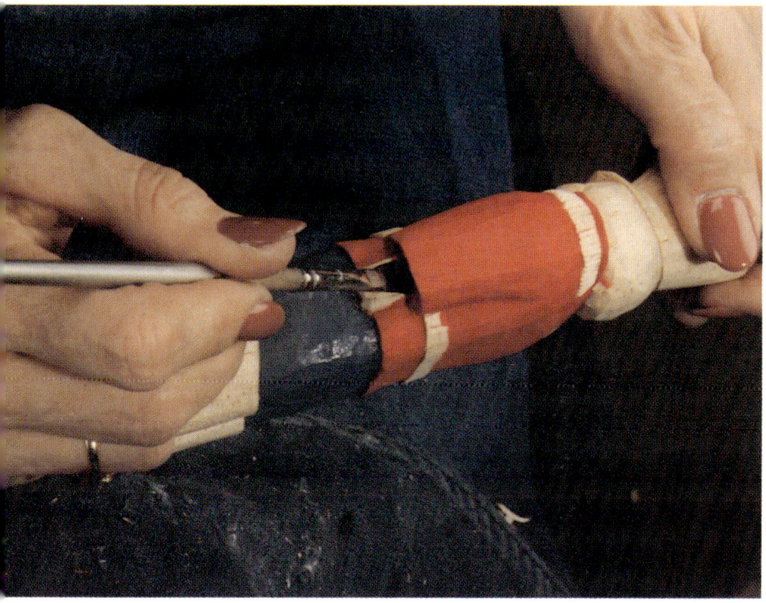

Black is used for the gloves...

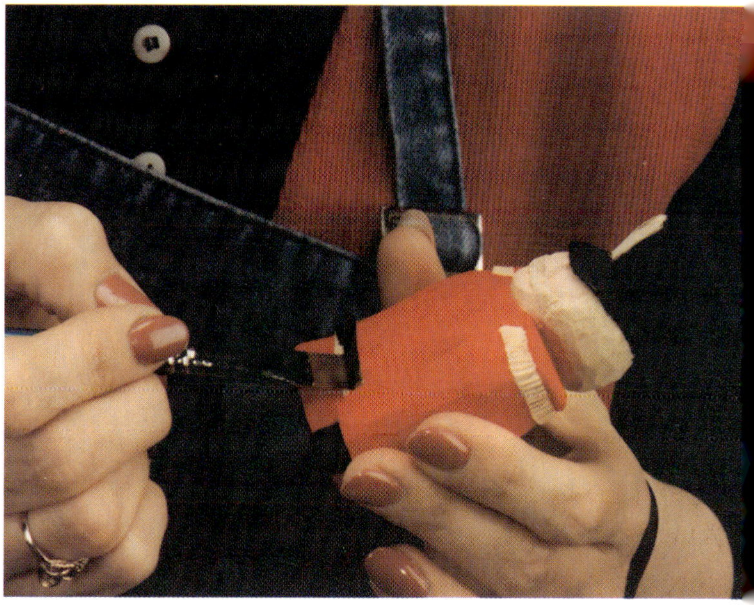

and the belt.

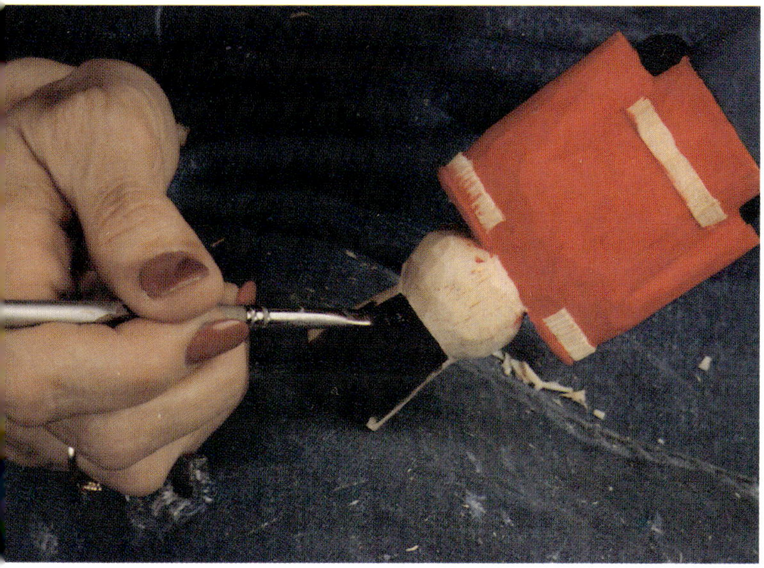

the hat...

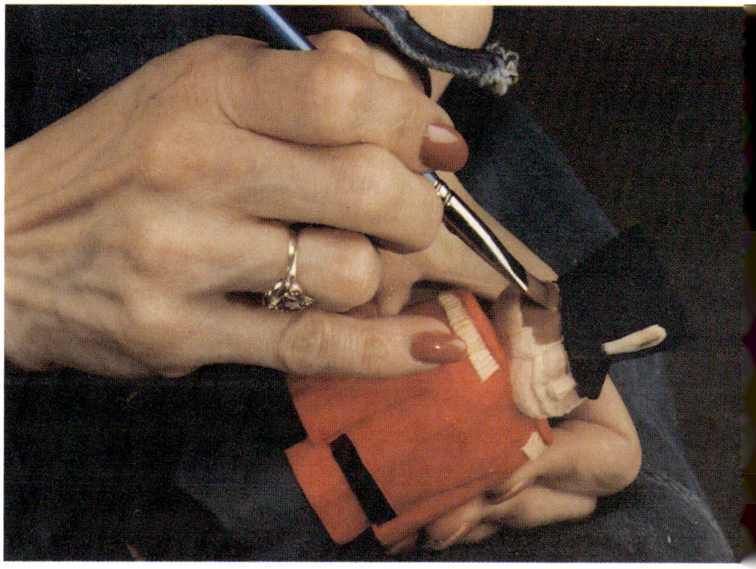

Paint the hair brown.

Corner load the brush with red for blush. This means you dip one corner of the brush in the paint...

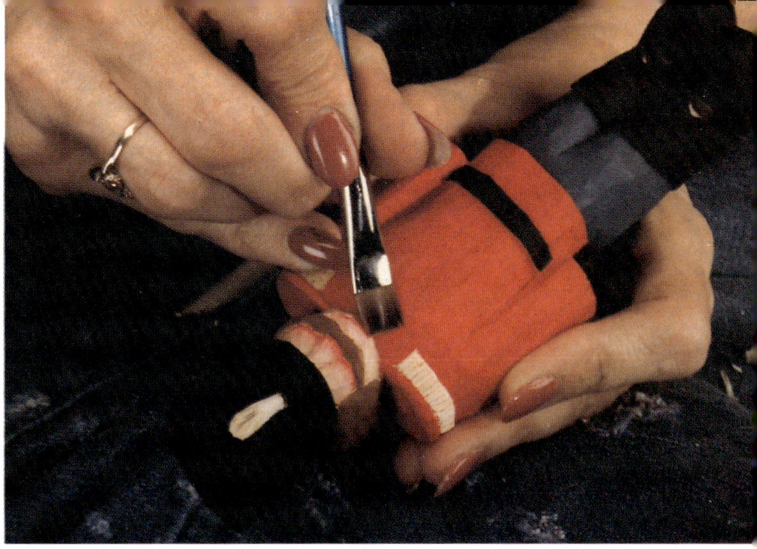

Also blush the chin, with the lightly loaded side of the brush against the moustache.

then work it on the palette so the pigment is graduated across the bristles going from heavy at the corner to light.

Progress.

With the heavy loaded corner against the moustache come across the cheeks and the nose.

Draw in the cross straps, front and back.

and the plume.

Paint the cross straps with warm gold.

Paint a gold buckle on the belt...

Also apply the gold to the fringe of the epaulets...

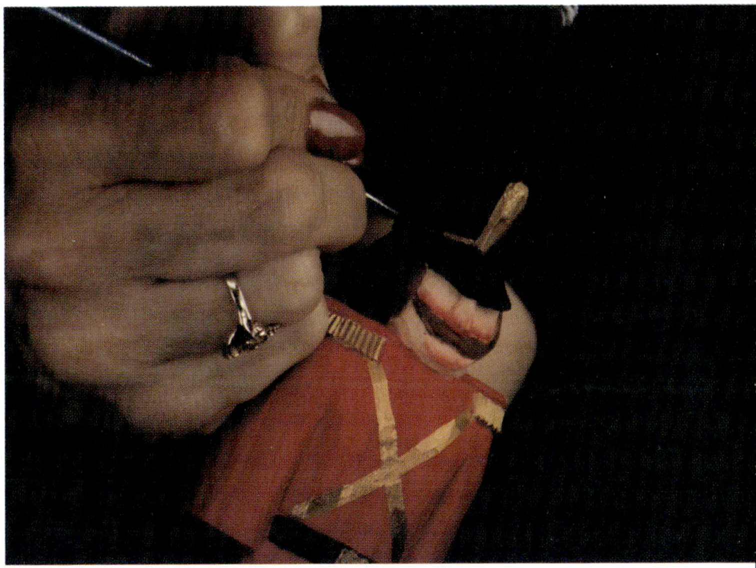

and add some decorative lines to the hat band...

around the top of the epaulets...

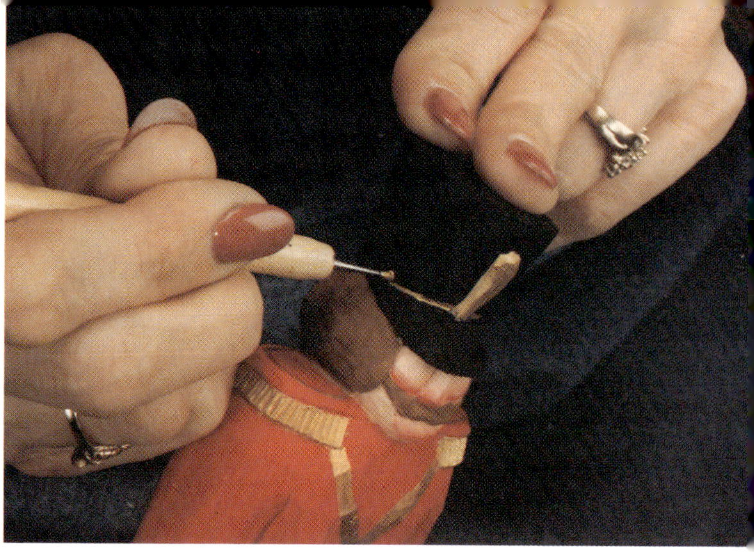

With a stylus or the pointed end of a brush make gold buttons at the ends of the hat band...

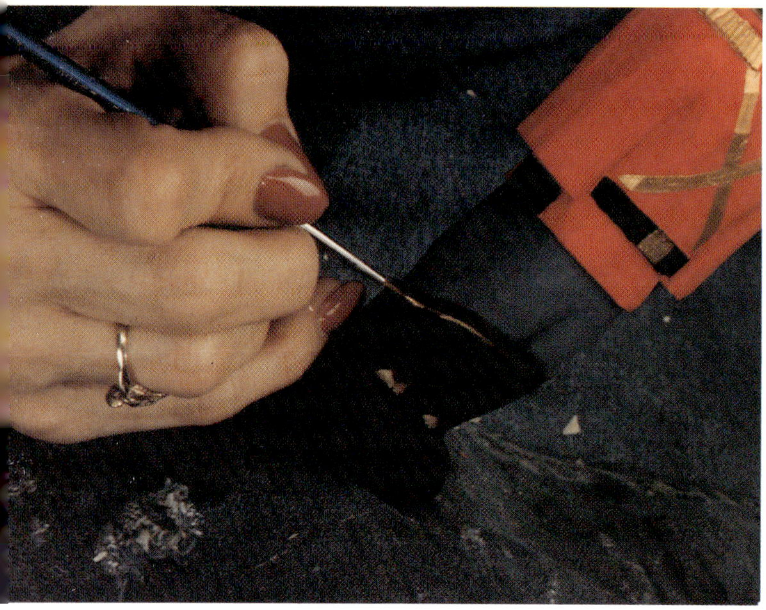

around the top of the boot...

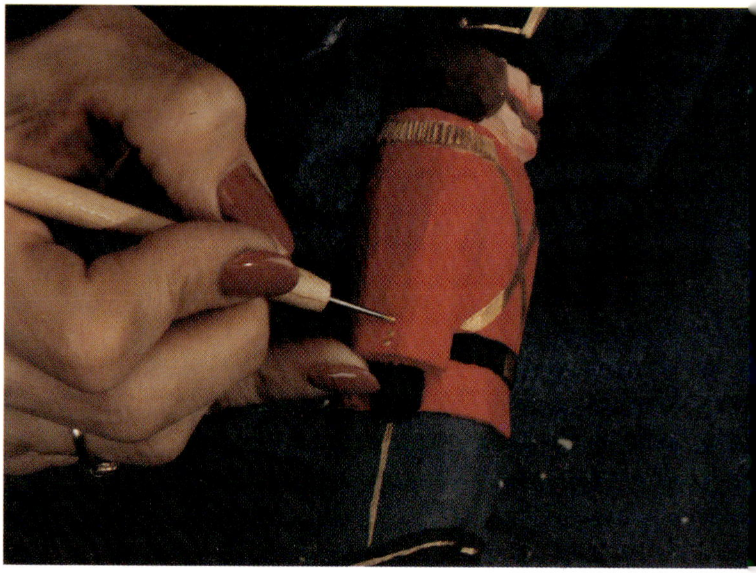

and on the sleeve.

and down the side of the pants.

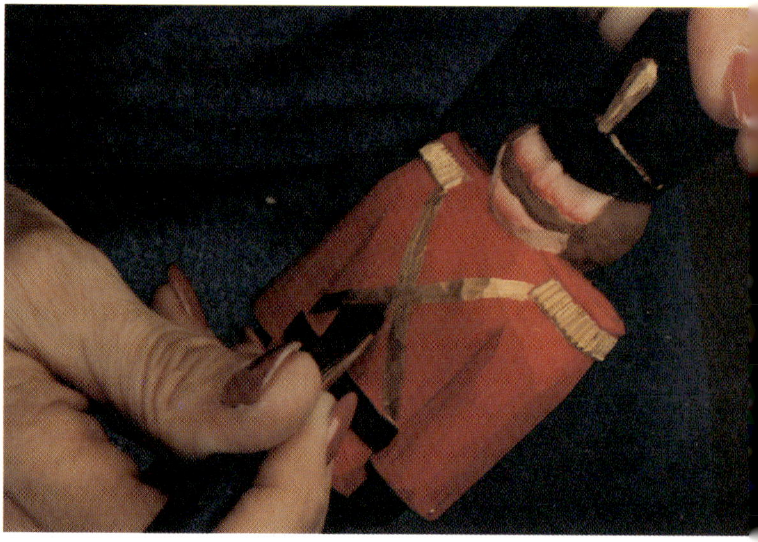

Corner load the brush with nutmeg and shade the strap where one goes under the other.

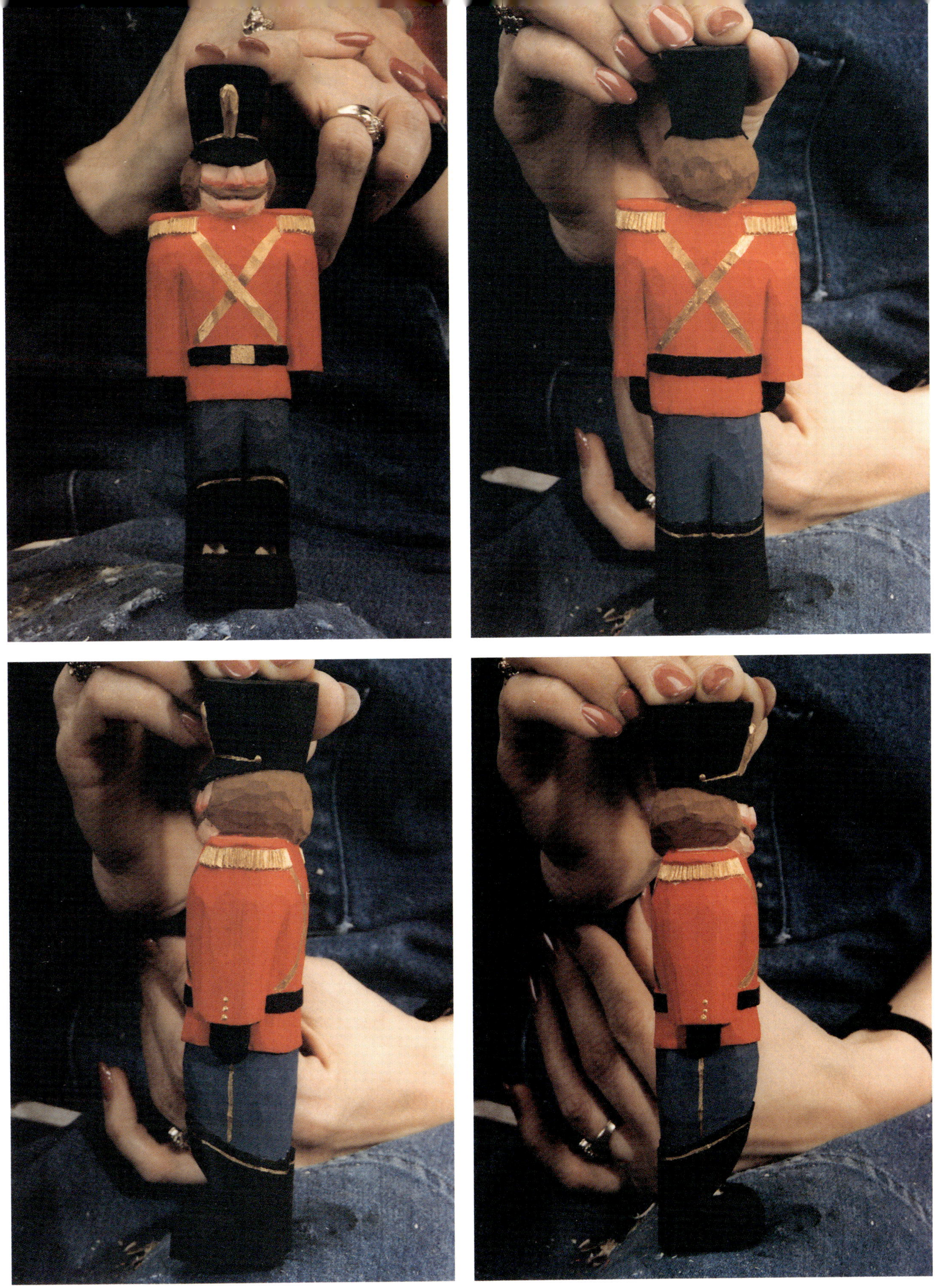

Ready for antiquing.

Painting Santa

Light Ivory

Peaches and Cream

Shammrock

Napthol Red Light

Black

Straw

Carve away the dowel so it is flush with the bottom.

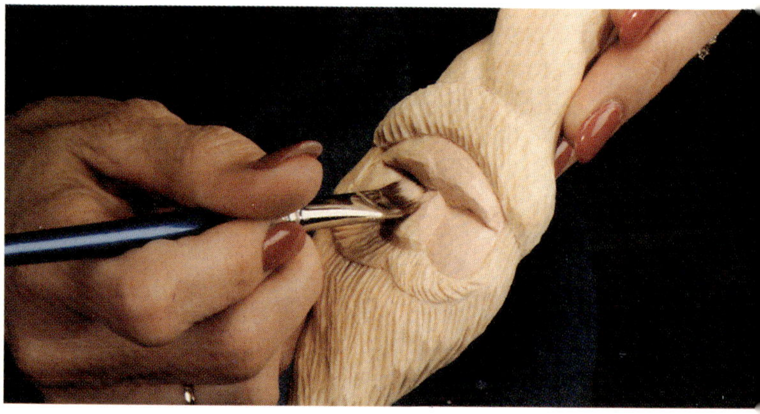

Paint the face of Santa with Peaches and Cream.

Apply light ivory to the fur...

the moustache and the beard.

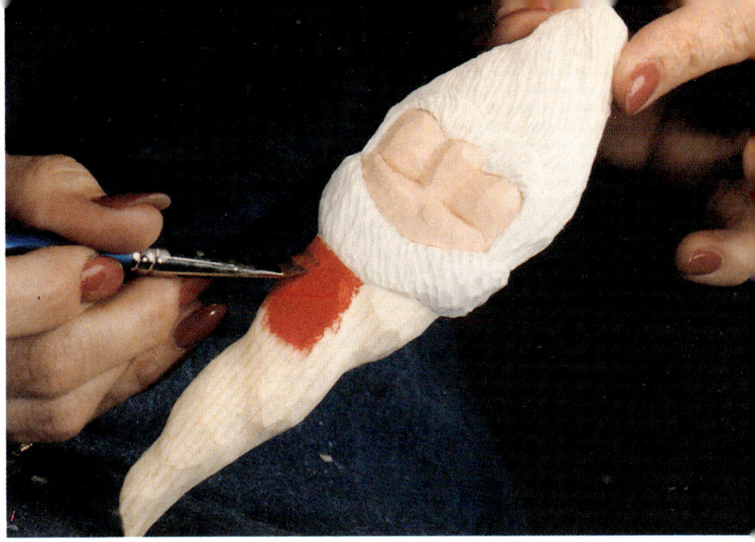

Paint the hat red.

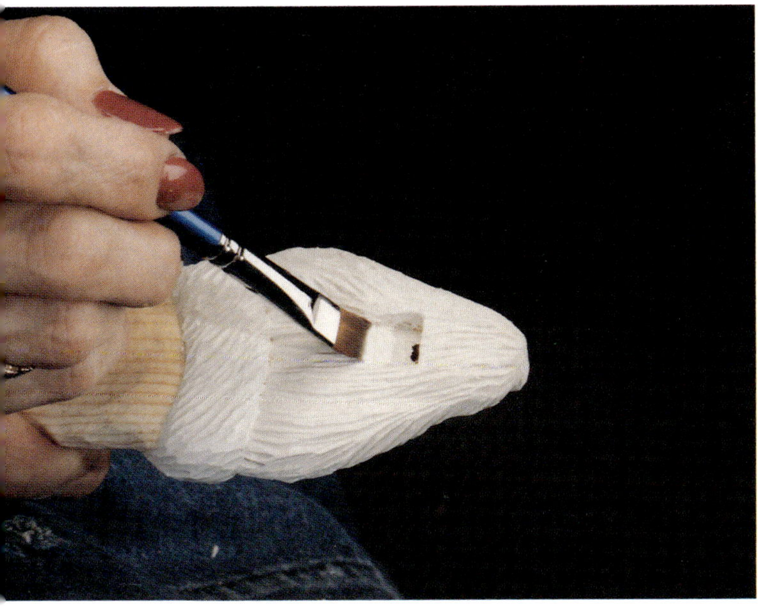

Be careful not to put too much paint on the reed.

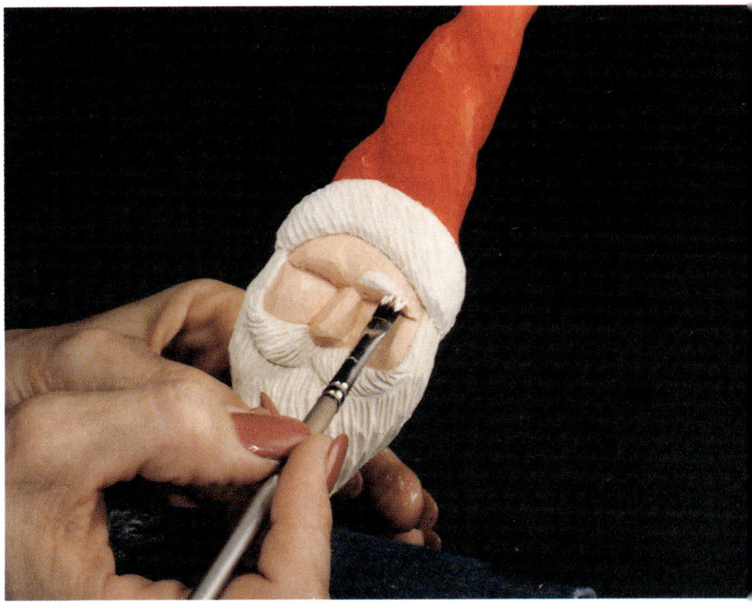

Dab the eyebrows with the light ivory.

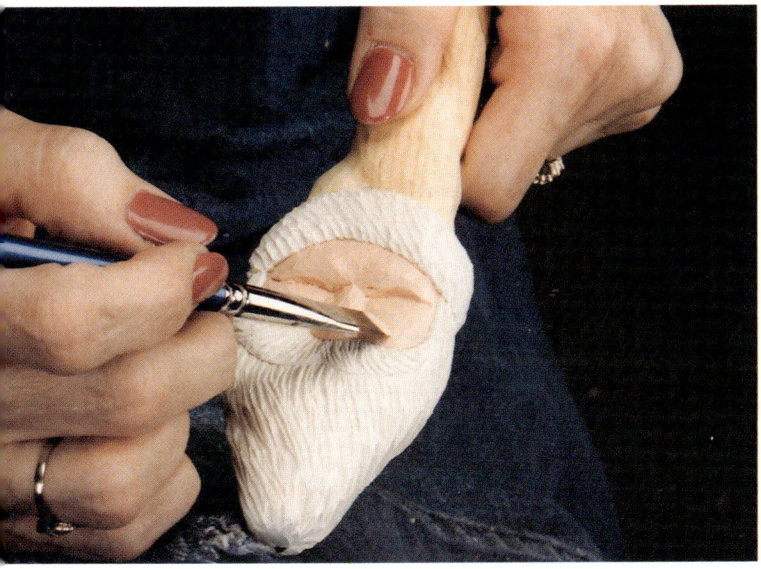

Add a second coat to the face.

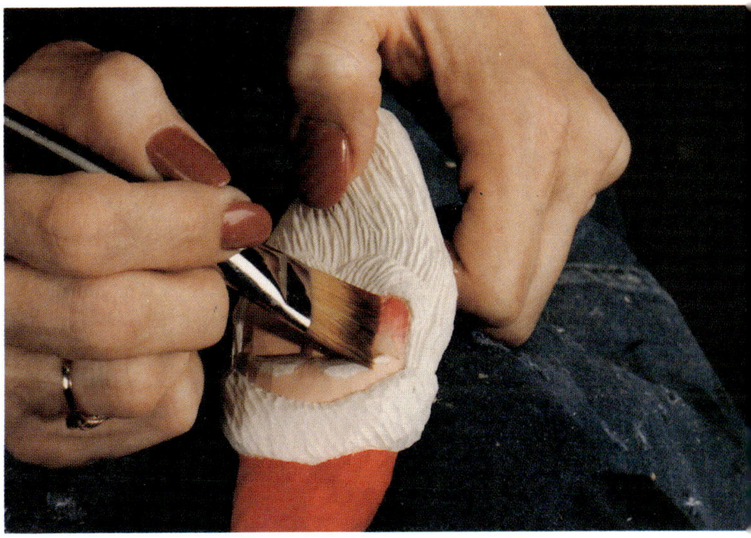

Corner load the brush with red and add blush to the cheek and nose. Keep the loaded edge against the hairline.

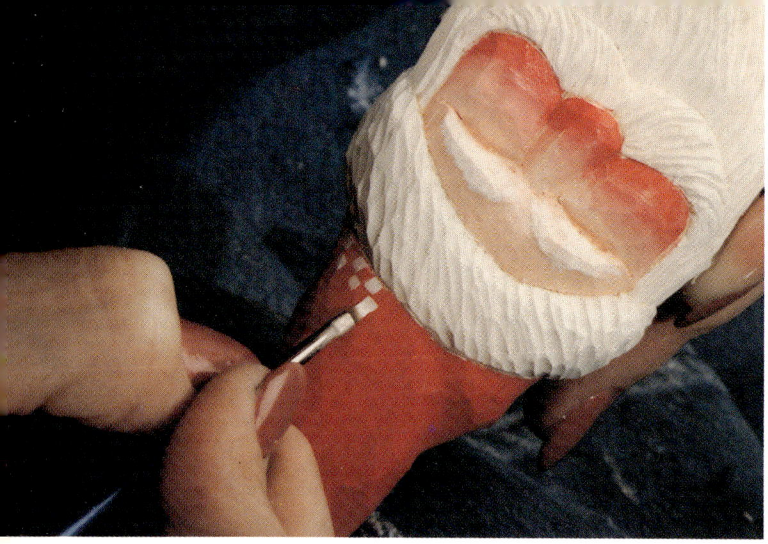

With a small chisel brush create a double checkerboard trim around the hat.

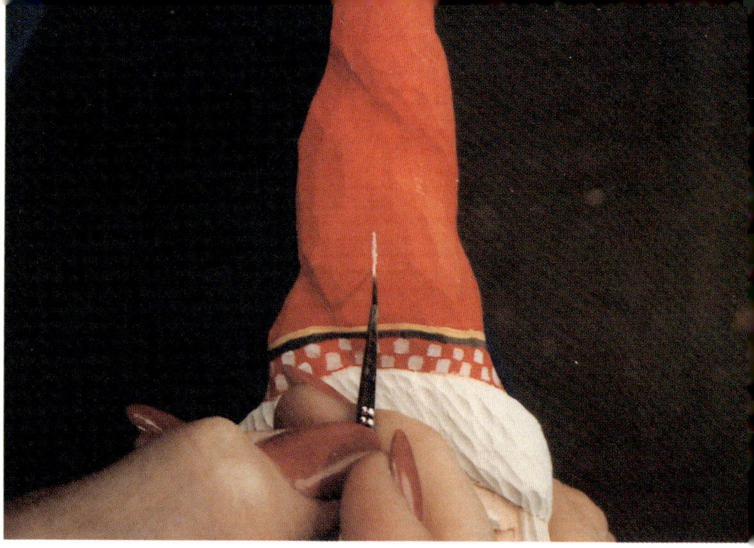

The stars on the hat are made with a fine liner brush. Begin with a vertical line.

Run a stripe of green above the checkerboard.

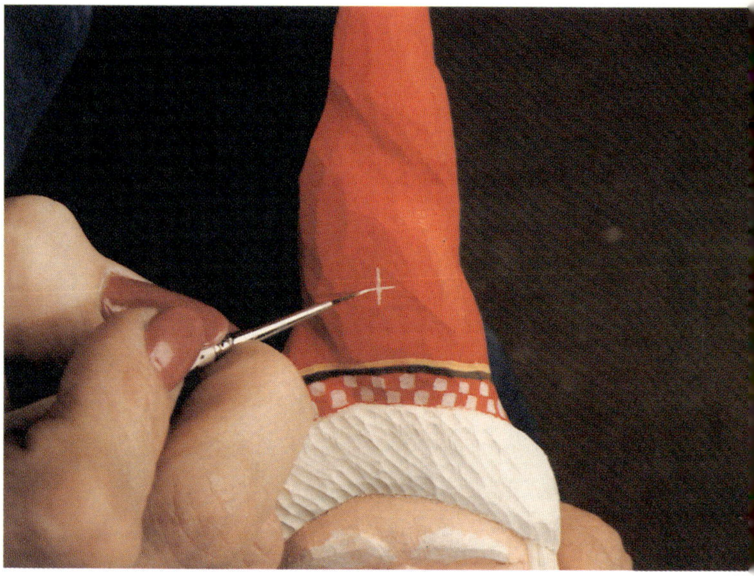

Add a horizontal line...

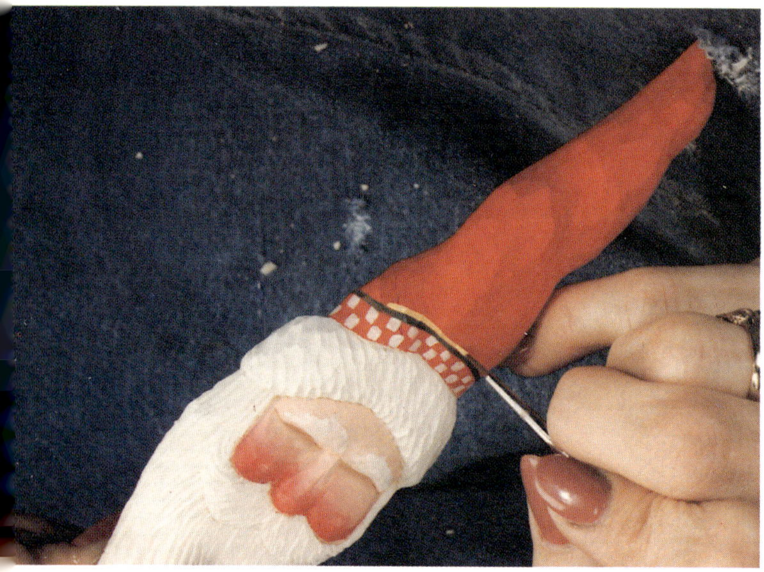

A stripe of Straw (yellow) runs above the green.

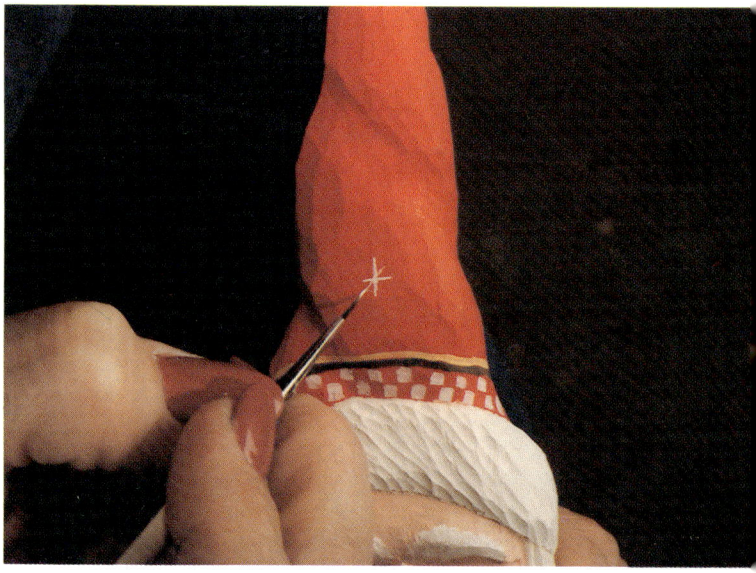

a diagonal one way...

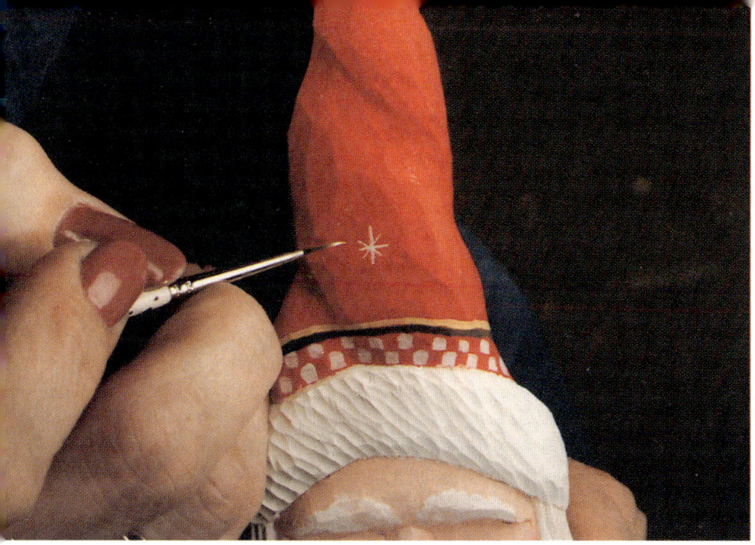

and another diagonal the other way.

Draw it out to one side...

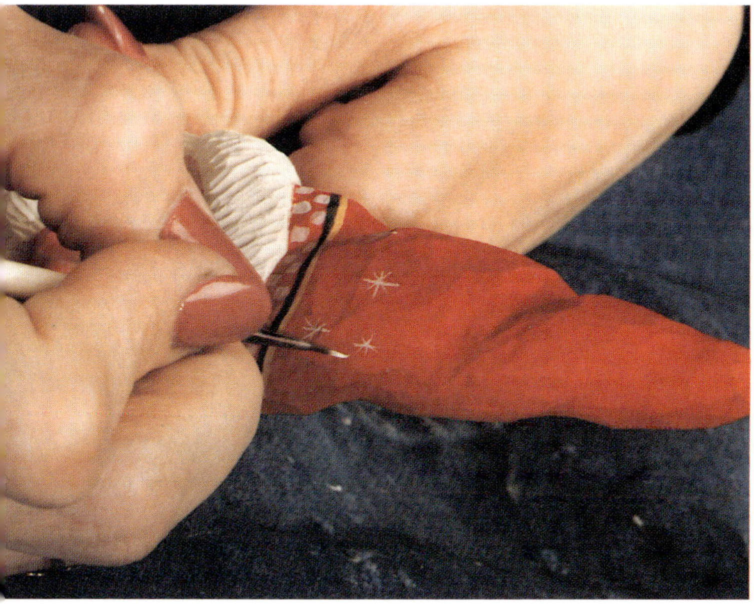

Repeat randomly over the hat.

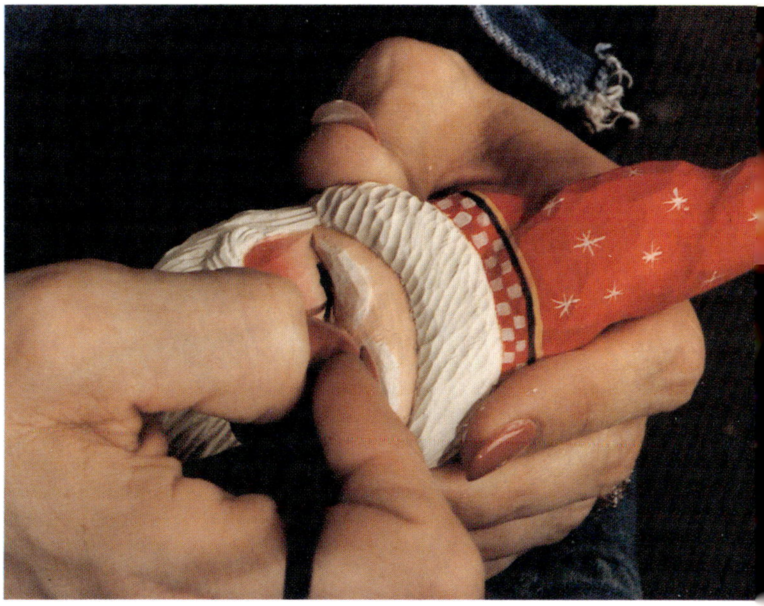

and the other.

To form the eyes, put a dot of black paint in the position of the iris.

Add a white dot in the same spot in each eye to give them life.

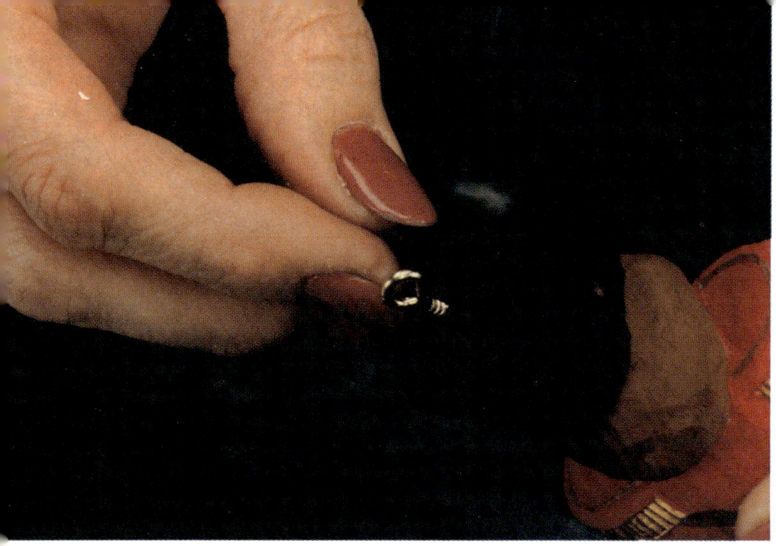

A brass eye screw in the top of the whistle allows it to hang on the Christmas tree as an ornament. Whenever possible put the screw at the opposite end from the blow hole. This makes it less likely that a child will accidentally swallow the hardware while playing with the toy.

In preparation for antiquing, apply several coats of a clear varnish or lacquer spray, allowing the finish to completely dry between coats.

The antiquing is done with burnt umber artist's oil, diluted with thinner to a consistency of melted chocolate chips. Cover the figure completely.

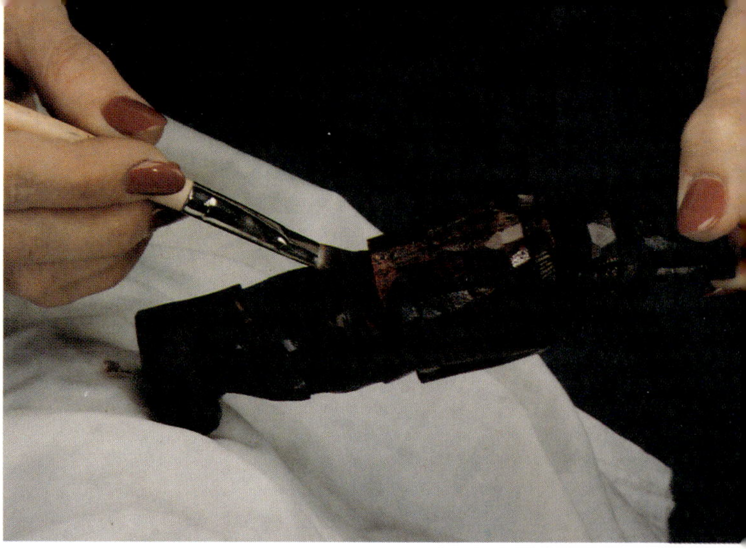

Remember to work the paint into hard to reach corners.

Thin the paint down until it has the watery consistency of a wash and apply it to the hole of the whistle.

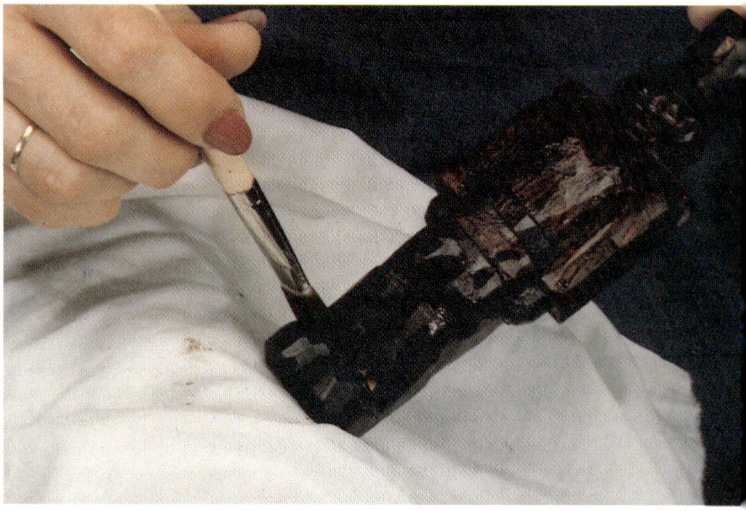

You want color but no paint build up that would interfere with the whistle.

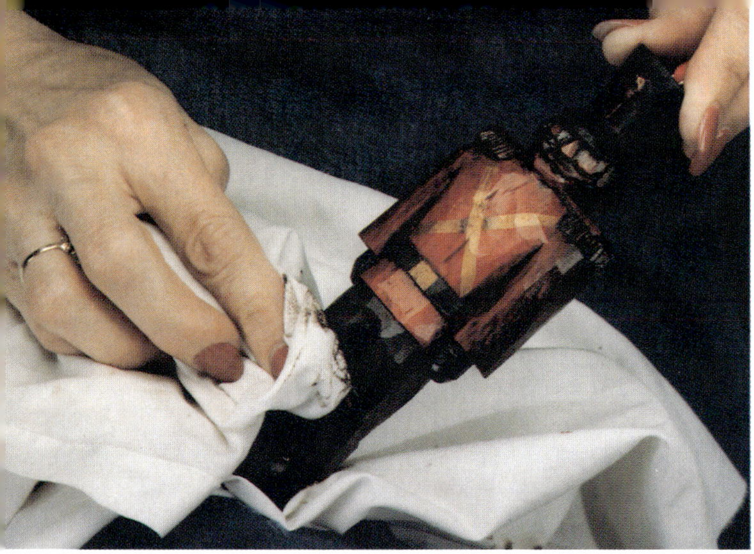

While the paint is still wet, remove it with paper toweling.

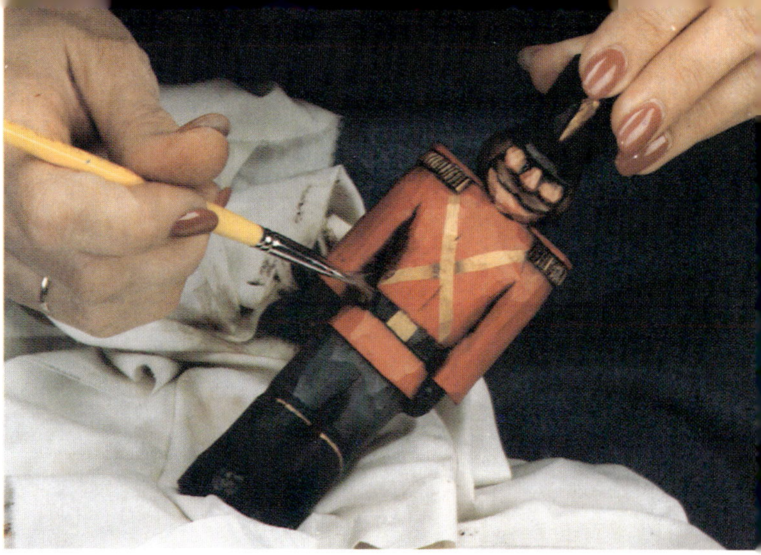

When most of the paint is removed use a dry soft brush to blend the heavy pigment out of the corners.

The result.

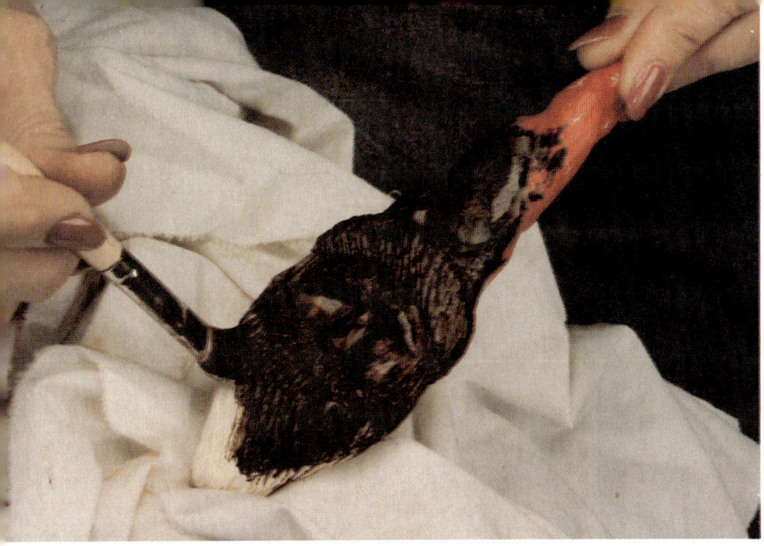

Use the same technique with the Santa whistle.

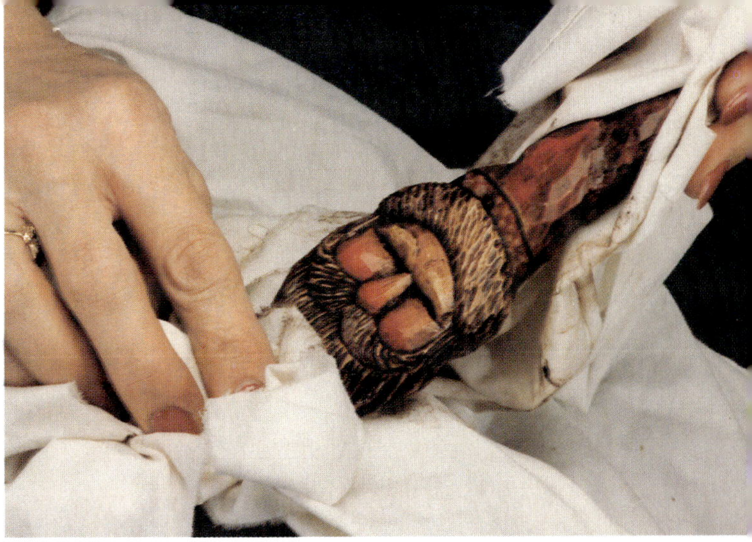

Wipe the brown away.

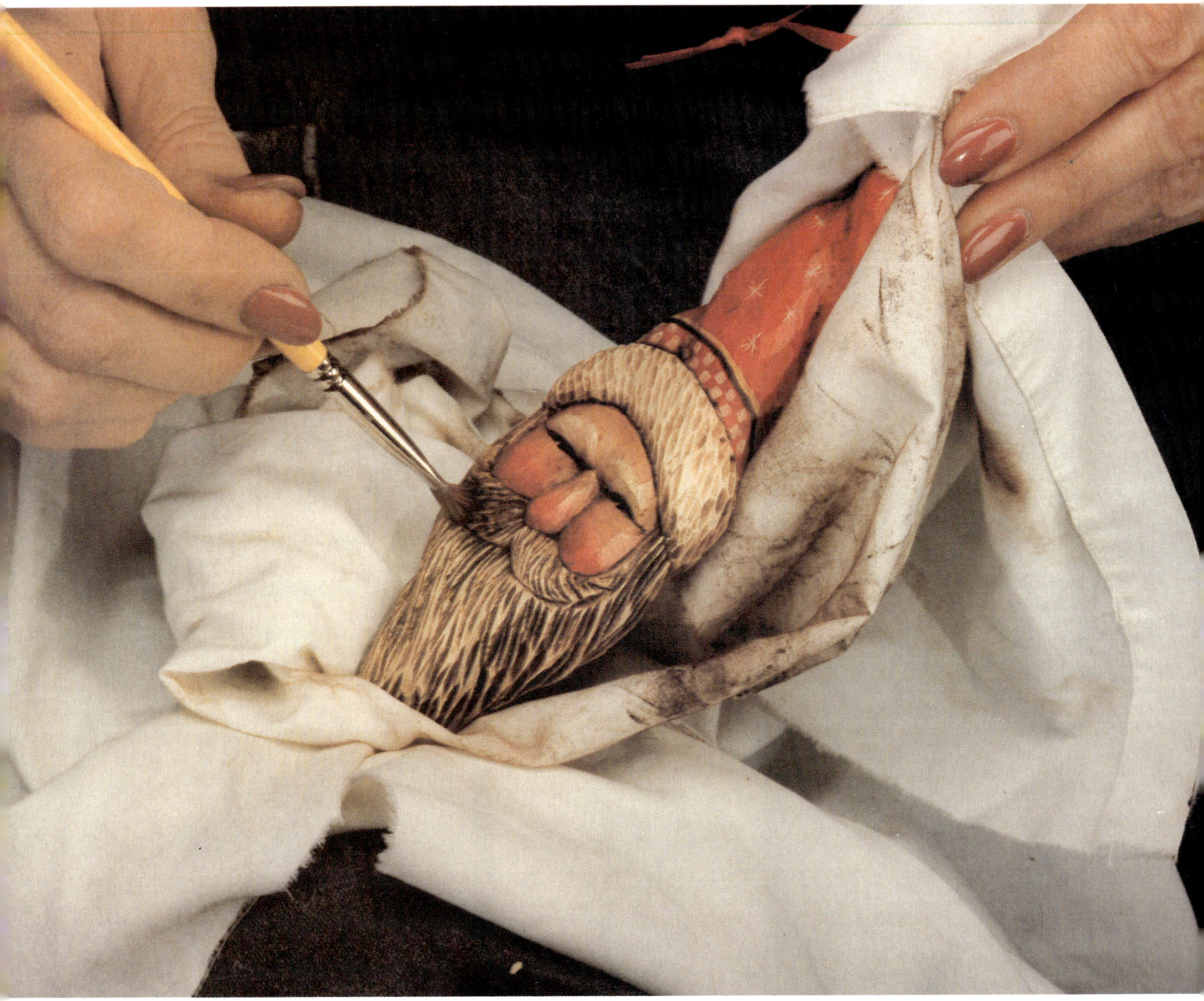

Clean out the crevices.

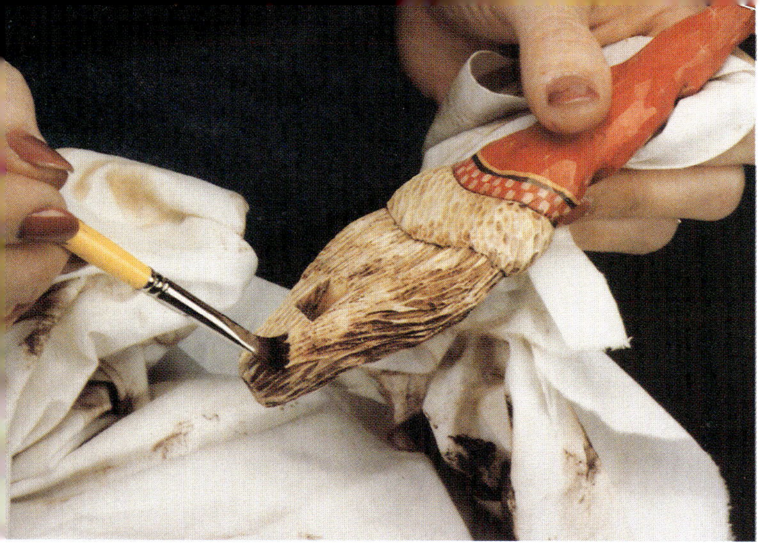

The beard area is a little dark so I'm going over it with a little bit of thinner to reduce the pigment.

Finished.

Allow the paint to dry for 48 hours, then add another light coat of wood finish.

Gallery and Patterns

© Kelley S. Stadelman

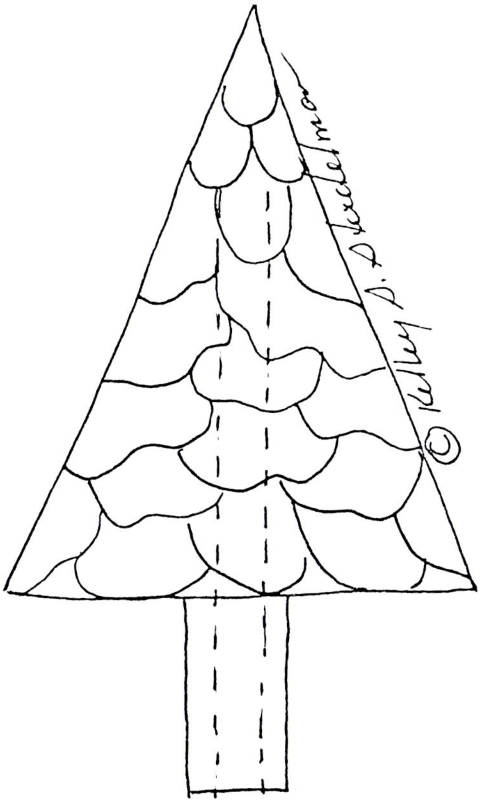
© Kelley D. Stadelman

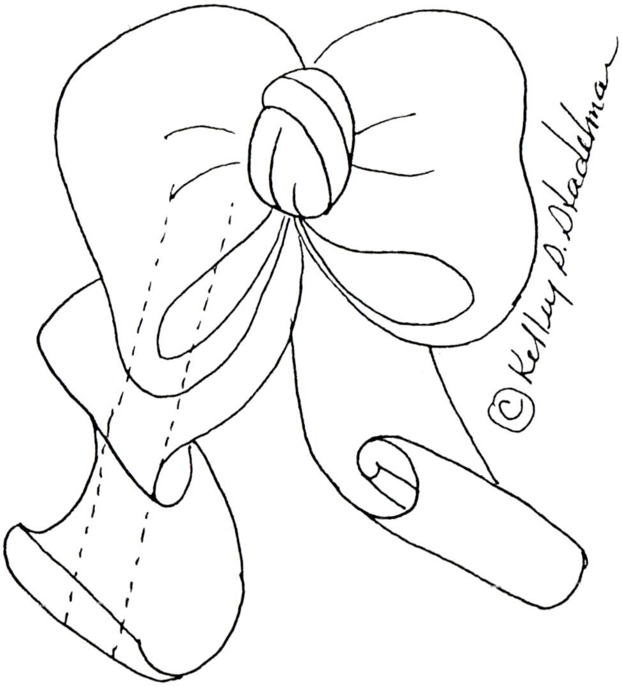
©Kelley P. Stadelman

© Kelley D. Stadelman

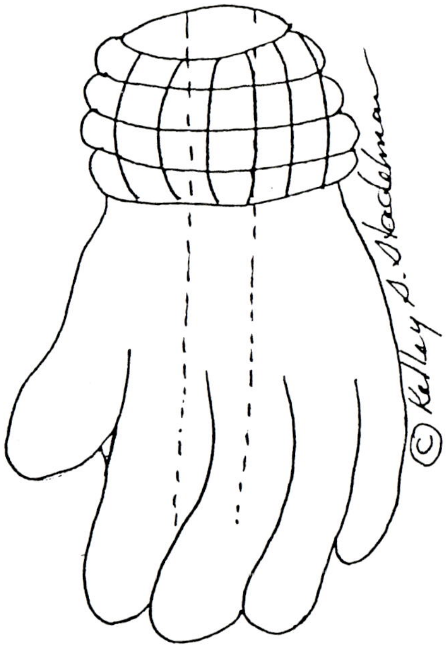
© Kelley S. Stadelman

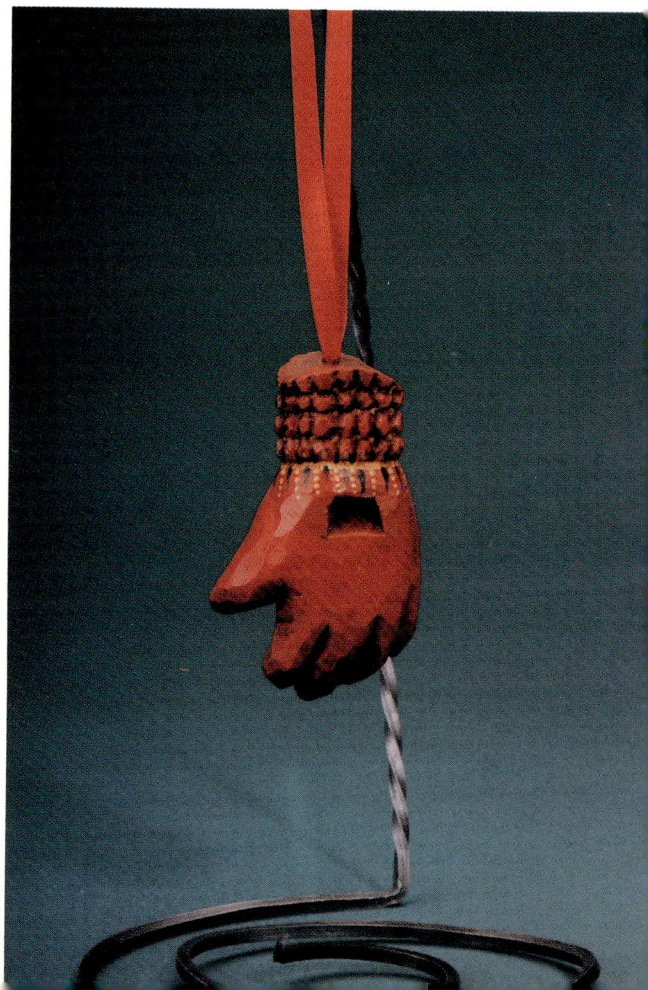

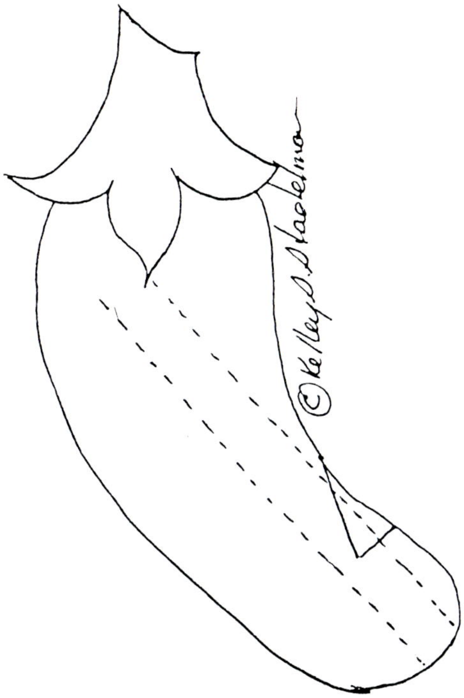
©Kelley S. Stadelman

©Kelley D. Stadelman

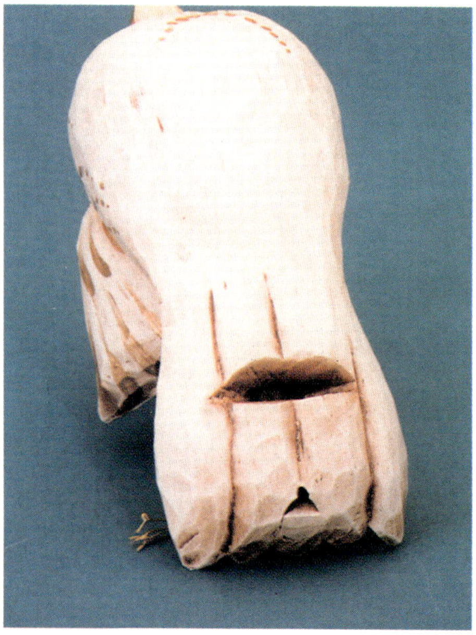

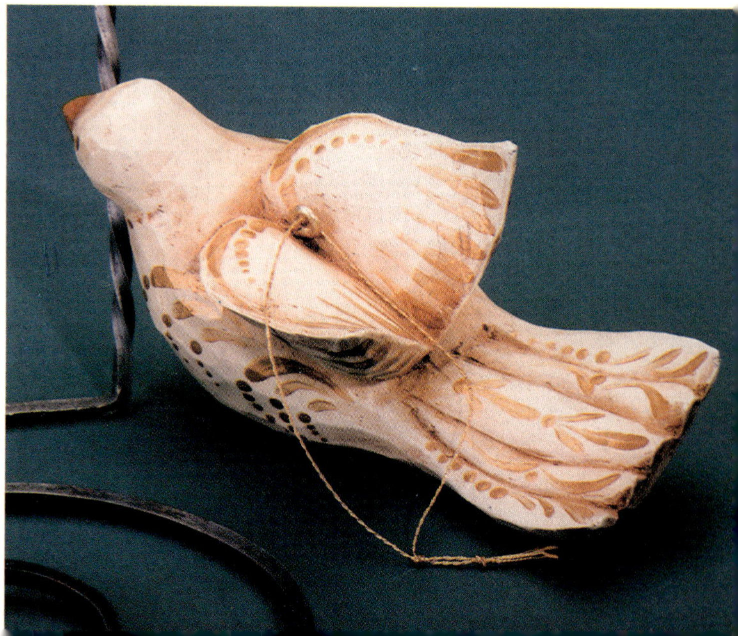

© Kelley D. Stadelman